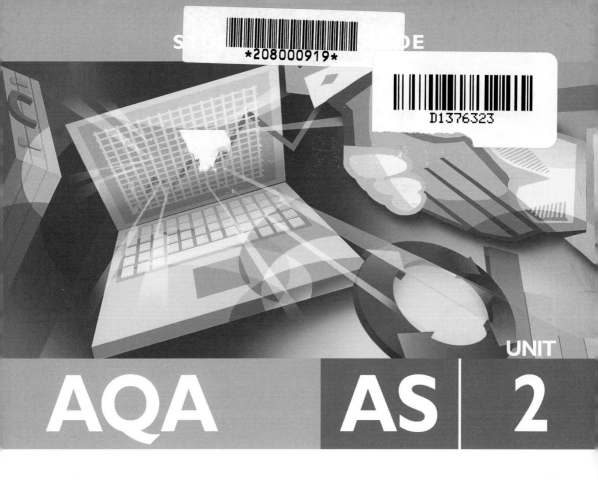

UNIT

AQA AS 2

Business Studies

Managing a Business

Isobel Rollitt-James

Series Editor: John Wolinski

Philip Allan Updates, an imprint of Hodder Education, an Hachette UK Company, Market Place, Deddington, Oxfordshire OX15 0SE

Orders

Bookpoint Ltd, 130 Milton Park, Abingdon, Oxfordshire OX14 4SB
tel: 01235 827720
fax: 01235 400454
e-mail: uk.orders@bookpoint.co.uk
Lines are open 9.00 a.m.–5.00 p.m., Monday to Saturday, with a 24-hour message answering service. You can also order through the Philip Allan Updates website: www.philipallan.co.uk

© Philip Allan Updates 2008

ISBN 978-0-340-95817-9

First printed 2008
Impression number 6
Year 2013 2012 2011 2010

This guide has been written specifically to support students preparing for the AQA AS Business Studies Unit 2 examination. The content has been neither approved nor endorsed by AQA and remains the sole responsibility of the author.

Typeset by DC Graphic Design, Swanley Village, Kent
Printed by MPG Books, Bodmin

Hachette UK's policy is to use papers that are natural, renewable and recyclable products and made from wood grown in sustainable forests. The logging and manufacturing processes are expected to conform to the environmental regulations of the country of origin.

Contents

Introduction

■ ■ ■

Content Guidance

■ ■ ■

Questions and Answers

Introduction

About this guide

This guide has been written with one objective in mind: to provide you with the ideal resource for your revision of AQA AS Business Studies Unit 2 (BUSS2): Managing a Business. After this introductory note on the aims and assessment of AS Business Studies, the guide is divided into two sections: Content Guidance and Questions and Answers.

The first section offers concise coverage of Unit 2, combining an overview of key terms and concepts with an identification of opportunities for you to illustrate the higher level skills of analysis and evaluation. The scope for linking different topic areas is also shown.

The second section provides four questions, which are focused on specific areas of content and in the same order as the first section. Questions 1 and 2 both combine 'Finance' and 'People in business', to reflect the fact that these will tend to be the first two elements of Unit 2 taught. Question 3 focuses solely on 'Operations management' and Question 4 covers 'Marketing and the competitive environment'. This section concludes with Questions 5 and 6. These are both fully integrated questions, for final revision purposes. Combined together Questions 5 and 6 take the format of an actual Unit 2 examination paper. Each question is based on the format of the AS papers and followed by two sample answers (an A-grade and a lower-grade response) interspersed by examiner comments.

You should read through the relevant topic area in the Content Guidance section before attempting the question from the Question and Answer section, and only read the specimen answers after you have tackled the question yourself. The Unit 2 examination consists of compulsory, multi-part data-response questions. The examination consists of two articles followed by a set of questions relating to that article. The time allocation for Unit 2 is 90 minutes (1 hour 30 minutes). Therefore, under examination conditions, each multi-part question in this guide should be completed in 45 minutes.

Aims of the AS qualification

AQA AS Business Studies aims to encourage candidates to develop a critical understanding of the following:
- the importance of entrepreneurial activity in the UK
- the issues involved in business start-ups, such as research and planning and sound financial management
- the factors that determine success in small and expanding businesses
- the internal functions of contemporary business organisations of all types

- how established businesses might improve their effectiveness by making tactical decisions at a functional level

In addition, the specification has been designed to encourage students to acquire a range of important and transferable skills, useful in both future employment and higher education:
- data skills — students will be expected to manipulate data in a variety of forms and to interpret their results
- presenting arguments and making judgements and justified recommendations on the basis of the available evidence
- recognising the nature of problems, solving problems and making decisions using appropriate business tools and methods
- planning work, taking into account the demands of the task and the time available to complete it
- conducting research into a specific theme in preparation for one and more tasks
- challenging their own assumptions using evidence that has become available

Unit 2 (BUSS2): Managing a business

Specifically, this unit examines the four functional areas of the business in relation to the core theme of improving the effectiveness of a business. It is intended to develop understanding of the importance of:
- the management of finance
- the management of human resources
- operations management
- the role of marketing in the competitive environment

These business functions are considered in terms of their impact upon the effectiveness of the business as assessed by measures such as profitability, labour productivity, labour turnover, unit costs and market share.

Assessment

AS and A2 papers are designed to test certain skills. **Every mark that is awarded on an AS or A2 paper is given for the demonstration of a skill.** The content of the course (the theories, concepts and ideas) provides a framework to allow students to show their skills — recognising the content on its own is not enough to merit high marks.

The following skills are tested:
- **Knowledge and understanding** — recognising and describing business concepts and ideas.
- **Application** — being able to explain or apply your understanding.

- **Analysis** — developing a line of thought in order to demonstrate its impact or consequences.
- **Evaluation** — making a judgement by weighing up the evidence provided.

Unit 2 is weighted so that, on average, marks for each question paper are awarded as follows:

	Weighting	
Knowledge	21	How well you know the meanings, theories and ideas
Application	19	How well you can explain benefits, problems, calculations, situations
Analysis	23	How well you develop ideas and apply theory and ideas to matters
Evaluation*	17	How well you show judgement, such as the overall significance of the situation
Total	80 marks	

* Marks awarded for evaluation incorporate an allocation of marks for quality of language.

Unit 2 has a higher weighting for the 'higher level' skills of analysis and evaluation. Bear this in mind during your preparation and revision for Unit 2 (BUSS2) as you will need to practise developing arguments more fully for this paper. This will also be good practice for the A2 papers that have a higher weighting for evaluation (but not for analysis). The units have been designed to allow you to develop skills, especially evaluation, as you progress through the course.

For the purposes of comparison the 60 marks awarded for the **Unit 1 (BUSS1)** paper are awarded as follows:

	Weighting	
Knowledge	21	How well you know the meanings, theories and ideas
Application	16/17	How well you can explain benefits, problems, calculations, situations
Analysis	12	How well you develop ideas and apply theory and ideas to matters
Evaluation*	10/11	How well you show judgement, such as the overall significance of the situation
Total	60 marks	

* Marks awarded for evaluation incorporate an allocation of marks for quality of language.

Skills requirement of a question

A rough guide to the skills requirement of a question is its mark allocation. For Unit 2 (90 minutes), 80 marks are available. After approximately 10 minutes for reading the text and the questions this is approximately a mark a minute — use this as a guide to the time you spend on each question, but allow some flexibility in your planning. For individual questions the mark allocation will tend to be as follows:

2–3 marks	A definition or description showing **knowledge***
3–6 marks	An explanation or calculation showing **application**
5–9 marks	Development of an argument in the context of the question showing **analysis**
10–15 marks	A judgement of a situation or proposed action showing **evaluation**

* It is possible, but unlikely, that a question will be set on this paper that only tests knowledge.

In the assessment of 'higher level' questions requiring analysis or evaluation, marks will also be given for the other skills. Factual knowledge displayed, for example, will earn marks for **knowledge** (content) and explanations and calculations will be awarded **application** marks.

A more specific guide to the skills requirement of a question is to look at the trigger word introducing the question. Specific trigger words are used to show you when you are being asked to analyse or evaluate. For AS, these are usually the following:

Analyse
- 'Analyse...'
- 'Explain why...'
- 'Examine...'
- 'Consider...'

Evaluate
- 'Evaluate...'
- 'Discuss...'
- 'To what extent...?'
- 'Justify...'

If these trigger words are missing on an AS paper, you are probably being asked to show 'lower level' skills, i.e. knowledge of the specification content or application (explanation).

On the Finance questions, the recall of a formula or method of calculation (e.g. break-even quantity) is knowledge. Carrying out calculations is application. This means that the high-mark questions that test analysis and evaluation do not usually involve calculations. Focus on understanding the purposes and limitations of the financial elements of the course and you will be well prepared for these questions. However, analysis questions may require you to interpret the meaning of a calculation.

Students who fail to **analyse** generally do so because they have curtailed their argument. The words and phrases below serve to provide logical links in an argument:
- 'and so...'

- 'which will mean/lead to...'
- 'because...'
- 'and this will affect...'

By using them you can demonstrate your ability to analyse. Always ask yourself: 'Am I explaining *why*?'

In order to **evaluate**, you need to demonstrate judgement and the ability to reach a reasoned conclusion. The following terms will demonstrate to the examiner that this is your intention:

- 'The most significant...is...because...'
- 'However, ...would also need to be considered because...'
- 'The probable result is...because...'
- 'On balance...because...'

The suggestions above are only a few of many ways in which judgements can be shown, but note the importance of the word 'because'.

Opportunities for evaluation in Unit 2

What follows is a summary of many of the probable opportunities for the demonstration of evaluation in Unit 2, although it is not an exhaustive list. The structure of the module and the nature of the topics mean that there are more opportunities in the Marketing than in the Finance part of the specification. The list does not include possibilities for evaluation that might arise from combining Marketing and Finance in an evaluative question. The nature of the topics means that there are many opportunities for evaluation that might arise also from combining the different functional areas, such as People in business and Operations management in evaluative questions.

Every business activity within operations management can influence 'people' aspects such as motivation and recruitment and training. Similarly, the personnel policies of an organisation will have implications for operations management. The summary below does not include the potential for this type of integration. In many instances, evaluation can be improved by referring to the effect of a people issue on the organisation's operations or vice versa.

Try to find a business problem within the scope of this module that does not integrate two or more functional areas.

Finance

- Usefulness of budgeting.
- Actions to be taken in response to budget variances.
- The most probable causes of budget variances.
- Value of delegation of budgets.

- Best ways to improve cash flow (in given circumstances).
- Decision on whether or not cash flow needs to be improved.
- Discussion of the relative importance of cash flow and profit in a given situation.
- Evaluation of whether a financial trend (e.g. cash flow or profit) is within a firm's control.
- Most probable causes of high or low profits for a specific business.
- Evaluation of methods a business might use to improve profits or profitability.

People in business

- Judgement based on the optimum choice of company structure (e.g. centralised or decentralised).
- Overall evaluation of the reasons for or the relative merits of or the implications of:
  – the number of levels of hierarchy
  – the span of control in a situation
  – a company decision on delayering
  – functional or matrix management
- Virtues of delegation or consultation in a situation.
- Assessment of the relative success or suitability of different measures used to improve motivation.
- Assessment of the effectiveness of the workforce.
- Comparison of recruitment methods.
- Pros and cons of the approach to staff training used by a business.
- Assessment of different training methods.

Operations management

- Overall judgement on the optimum size of a business in terms of operational efficiency.
- Evaluation of the reliability or significance of different measures of operational efficiency.
- Assessment of the quantitative and qualitative factors that affect unit costs (or an alternative measure of operational efficiency).
- Assessment of the causes of under-utilising capacity.
- Assessment of the consequences of under-utilising capacity.
- Evaluation of the best way to improve use of capacity (e.g. rationalisation or subcontracting).
- Evaluation of the consequences of employing methods to improve capacity utilisation.
- Overall assessment of the productivity and flexibility provided by a company's methods.
- Assessing the link between unit costs and people management.
- Judgement on the relative merits of quality control (inspection) and quality assurance (self-checking) in a particular scenario.

- Significance of quality to a firm.
- Usefulness of a quality standard to a firm.
- Possible issues arising from introducing a quality system.
- Main benefits from providing good customer service.
- Judgement on the factors that lead to good customer service for a specific business.
- Assessing the main factors influencing the choice of a supplier.
- Evaluation of the ways in which a supplier can help a business to reach its operational targets.
- The overall impact of technology on a business.
- Contrasting differences between the short-term and long-term implications of new technology in a particular situation.

Marketing and the competitive environment

- Evaluating the main purposes of marketing in a particular scenario.
- Recommendations on how to use product differentiation in mass marketing.
- Relative merits and demerits of niche marketing.
- Problems of using the product life cycle stages for marketing a product or product portfolio.
- The overall usefulness of the concept of the product life cycle to a given organisation.
- The usefulness of product portfolio analysis (e.g. through the Boston matrix).
- Choosing the best extension strategies.
- The merits of a particular change to the marketing mix.
- The link between successful (or unsuccessful) marketing and a change to one of the four Ps.
- Marketing mix judgements linked to other elements (e.g. market research data).
- Significance of factors that influence all or particular elements of the marketing mix (e.g. influences on price, promotion and so on).
- The application of price elasticity of demand information to a particular scenario.
- The usefulness of price elasticity of demand data in a particular case.
- Assessment of the importance of place to a particular marketing mix.
- The impact of the level of competition on the business's success.
- Judgement of the key factors that have led to a change in the firm's competitiveness.

Revision strategies

Below is a list of general pieces of advice for exam preparation.
- Prepare well in advance.
- Organise your files, ensuring there are no gaps.

- Prepare a list of key terms/definitions in readiness for the exam. Defining a term in an exam immediately shows that you understand the concept or topic and it can help to clarify your arguments.
- Read different approaches — there is no one right approach to business studies. Experience as many views and methods as possible. Read newspapers and business articles.
- When reading an article, try to think of the types of questions an examiner might ask and how you would answer them. Remember, some of your examination questions will be based on actual organisations.
- Take notes as you read. These will help you to:
  - put the text into your own words, cementing your understanding
  - summarise and emphasise the key points
  - focus your attention
  - précis information which could help with future revision
  - boost your morale by showing an end product of your revision sessions
- Develop and use your higher level skills. Make sure that your revision is not dominated by factual knowledge only. Check that you can explain and analyse the points noted, and try to imagine situations in which evaluation can be applied.
- Practise examination questions. Use the questions in this book (and specimen and past papers from the AQA website) to improve your technique, making sure that you complete them in the time allowed. In the Unit 2 examination you must complete two multi-part questions in 90 minutes, so allow 45 minutes per question. Time management is vital. A 90-minute examination paper means that there is a reasonable but finite amount of time to develop your answers. You *must* make sure that you have enough time to evaluate the final part of question 2. Remember that, within a question, the later parts carry more marks and therefore need longer, more fully developed answers. Remember, after reading time the 80 marks awarded approximate to 1 mark per minute. Use this as a guide to the time you need to spend on a particular question.
- Maintain your motivation. Reward yourself for achieving targets, but do not get demoralised if you fall behind. If necessary, amend your objectives to a more realistic level.
- Find out the dates and times of your examinations and use this to prepare a detailed schedule for the study leave/examination period, making sure you build in time for relaxation and sleep.
- Focus on all areas of the specification rather than just your favourite topics. Your revision is more likely to 'add value' if it improves your understanding of a problem area. Revising a topic that you already know is a morale booster, but is it as valuable?
- Top up your memory just before the examination. If there are concepts, formulae or ratios that you find difficult, revisit them just before the examination.
- Adopt your own strategies. Everyone has different learning styles — use the approach or methods that work for you.

Content
Guidance

This section of the guide outlines the topic areas of Unit 2 which are as follows:

- Finance
- People in business
- Operations management
- Marketing and the competitive environment

Read through the relevant topic area before attempting a question from the Question and Answer section.

Analysis

Under this heading, there are suggestions on how topic areas could lend themselves to analysis. During your course and the revision period you should refer to these opportunities. Test and practise your understanding of the variety of ways in which a logical argument or line of reasoning can be developed.

Evaluation

Under this heading, general opportunities for evaluation are highlighted within particular topic areas. A wide range of 'Opportunities for evaluation' are described in the Introduction.

Integration

The scope for linking different topic areas is shown under the heading 'Links'. Most business problems have many dimensions and a student who can show, for example, the effect of a marketing problem on a company's finances or its people management will be rewarded. Look for these opportunities to integrate. The introduction to Unit 2 states 'candidates should examine the topic areas below in relation to the core theme of improving the effectiveness of a business'. Use this core theme to integrate the four functional areas of an organisation, showing how each can contribute towards improving the overall efficiency of the business.

Finance

Using budgets

A budget is an agreed plan establishing in numerical or financial terms the policy to be pursued and the anticipated outcomes of that policy. Budgets are usually stated in terms of financial targets, relating to money allocated to support the organisation of a particular function, but they also include targets for revenue and output or sales volume. The key types of budget are:

- **income budget.** This shows the agreed, planned income of a business (or division of a business) over a period of time. It may also be described as a revenue budget or sales budget.
- **expenditure budget.** This shows the agreed, planned expenditure of a business (or division of a business) over a period of time.
- **profit budget.** This shows the agreed, planned profit of a business (or division of a business) over a period of time.

Benefits of using budgets

A budget may be used to bring the following benefits to an organisation:

- **To establish priorities** by indicating the level of importance attached to a particular policy or division.
- **To provide direction and coordination** by ensuring that spending is geared towards the firm's aims.
- **To assign responsibility** by identifying the person who is directly responsible for any success or failure.
- **To motivate staff** by giving them greater responsibility and recognition when they meet targets.
- **To improve efficiency** by investigating reasons for failure and success.
- **To encourage forward planning** by studying possible outcomes.

Drawbacks of using budgets

Certain undesirable consequences may occur, especially if the budgets are too rigid. Factors that may affect the efficacy of a budget include:

- **Incorrect allocations.** A budget that is too generous may encourage inefficiency. A budget that is insufficient will demotivate staff and hinder progress through a lack of money.
- **External factors.** Changes outside the budget holders' control may affect their ability to stick to the plan.
- **Poor communication.** Budgets must be agreed between people who understand the area in question and also other factors that might influence the budgets.

Budgetary control

Budgetary control is the establishment of the budget and the continuous comparison of actual and budgeted results in order to ascertain variances from the plan and to provide a basis for revision of the objective or strategy.

Variance analysis

A variance represents the difference between the planned standard and the actual performance. If the variance reveals a poorer performance than planned, it is known as an **adverse** or **unfavourable variance**, e.g. higher costs or lower sales revenue. If the variance shows a better performance than planned, it is known as a **favourable variance**, e.g. lower costs or higher sales revenue.

Identification of the cause of a variance can allow a company to:
- identify responsibility
- take appropriate action

For an adverse variable, providing the factor that caused it is under the firm's control, alternative methods can be investigated. Favourable variances can be used to identify efficient methods that can be adopted more widely in the company.

Causes of variances
Variances in costs can be caused by changes in:
- storage and wastage of material
- material costs (cheaper or dearer)
- efficiency changes
- morale and efficiency of staff
- wages
- quality of material

Interpretation of variances
The following table shows how variances can be interpreted as being either favourable or adverse. In the variance column, (F) indicates a favourable variance and (A) an adverse variance.

Identity of budget	Planned	Actual	Variance
Cost of sales			
Materials	10,000	12,000	2,000 (A)
Wages	15,000	14,000	1,000 (F)
Overheads			
Admin. staff	4,000	8,000	4,000 (A)
Rent and rates	5,000	7,000	2,000 (A)
Marketing	6,000	1,000	5,000 (F)
Other costs	5,000	5,000	Nil
Total costs	45,000	47,000	2,000 (A)

Analysis Account for the variances to the planned budgets shown in the budget table above, indicating apparent areas of efficiency and inefficiency. Use the list of six factors to identify possible causes.

Tip Variances may be caused by the firm (internally) or external factors. It is often easier to identify external changes (e.g. high inflation, shortages of materials) than internal ones.

Analysis Analysis may also take the form of showing the:
- implications of budget variances
- benefits of budgeting to the firm
- difficulties and problems of budgeting

Evaluation Possible approaches to evaluation in this area of the specification are to:
- identify the key causes of variances
- assess the best solutions to adverse variances
- judge the usefulness of budgeting, the difficulties of projecting and so on
- evaluate the pros and/or cons of profit centres and cost centres
- discuss the feasibility of solving problems

Budgets imply control — you may be able to focus on the style of manager who would support these processes.

Note: A major limitation of budgets is the timing. Budgets are set before the event and so people are guessing what will happen in the future. Variances are assessed after the event, by which time the problems have passed.

Improving cash flow

Cash-flow management involves careful control of cash in the short term in order to ensure **liquidity** (the ability of a firm to meet its short-term debts). A business sustaining losses will fail, but even a profitable firm can fold if it is unable to pay a creditor who requires payment in cash.

Cash-flow forecast

Too much cash means a firm will have less machinery and stock than it can afford and so makes less profit. Too little cash will threaten survival if a bill cannot be paid. In order to maintain the right balance, a firm plans its cash holdings by compiling a cash-flow forecast. This enables the organisation to identify potential problems and take appropriate action (e.g. arranging a bank overdraft).

Analysis You should be aware of the factors that can cause inaccurate cash-flow projections and/or the consequences of poor forecasting. However, analysis should focus on the management of cash flow or the causes of or solutions to cash-flow problems.

Causes of cash-flow problems

The main causes of cash-flow problems are:

- **over-investment** in fixed assets, leaving no money to pay bills
- **overtrading** — producing too many goods and running out of cash
- **credit sales** — increasing sales and thus expenses, but with no cash received until a later date
- **stockpiling** — tying up assets in stock
- **seasonal factors** — low sales revenue or high costs during part of the year
- **changing tastes** — products do not sell
- **management errors** — poor market research or budgetary control leading to cash shortages

Methods of improving cash flow

Cash flow can be improved by the following methods.

Bank overdraft

The benefits of an overdraft are:

- It is easy to organise.
- It is very flexible.
- It is often cheaper than a loan, because interest is paid only on the amount overdrawn and for the time when the overdraft is used.

The drawbacks of an overdraft are:

- Interest rates are flexible, making it difficult to budget accurately.
- The rate of interest charged on an overdraft is usually significantly higher than that charged on a short-term bank loan, so it can be more expensive.

Short-term loan/bank loan

The benefits are:

- Bank loans are usually made at a fixed rate of interest, making it simple to budget the loan repayments.
- The rate of interest charged on a bank loan is usually less than that charged on an overdraft, so it can be a cheaper solution to a cash-flow problem.
- A bank loan may be set up for a significant period of time to suit the needs of the business.

The drawbacks are:

- Interest is paid on the whole of the sum borrowed. If the business can repay the loan earlier, a loan penalty charge may be imposed.
- The business will need to provide the bank with security (collateral) in order to secure the loan.

Factoring (debt factoring)

Factoring is when a company (usually a bank) buys the right to collect the money from the credit sales of an organisation.

The benefits of factoring are:
- The firm gains improved cash flow in the short term.
- Administration costs are lower because the factoring company chases any bad debts.
- There is a reduced risk of bad debts.

The drawbacks of factoring are:
- The main problem is the cost to the business, which will lose between 5% and 10% of its revenue.
- The factoring company will charge more for factoring than it would for a loan.
- Customers may prefer to deal directly with the business that sold them the product.

Sale of assets

This process can improve cash flow by converting an asset, such as property or machinery, into cash which can then be used to ease the cash-flow problem by repaying a debt or building up a bank balance.

The benefits are:
- The sale of fixed assets can raise a considerable sum of money, particularly in the case of a large asset such as a building.
- Sometimes the asset may no longer be needed and is just adding to costs unnecessarily.

The drawbacks are:
- Assets such as buildings and machinery may be difficult to sell quickly.
- Fixed assets enable a firm to produce the goods and services that create its profit.

Evaluation Sale of assets is most likely to be used as a means of overcoming cash-flow problems when a business is seeking to get rid of an unprofitable part of the business that may actually be causing the problems in the first place.

Sale and leaseback of assets

Assets that are owned by the firm are sold to raise cash and then rented back so that the company can still use them for an agreed period of time.

The benefits are:
- This will overcome the cash-flow problem by providing an immediate inflow of cash, usually of quite a significant level.
- Ownership of fixed assets can lead to a number of costs, such as maintenance. For leased assets, the company leasing them does not have to pay these costs.
- Owning an asset can distract a business from its core activity.

The drawbacks are:
- The rent paid is likely to exceed the sum received, eventually.
- The firm now owns fewer assets that can be used as security against future loans.
- The business may eventually lose the use of the asset when the lease ends.

Integration opportunities

A firm can also improve its cash flow in the following ways:
- Diversifying its product portfolio to create a range that sells throughout the year.
- Anticipating change better through improved decision-making procedures, planning, monitoring and control, and more thorough market research and intelligence.
- Setting aside a contingency fund to allow for unexpected payments or cope with lost income.
- Controlling stock carefully to reduce the costs incurred in holding too much.

> **Evaluation** Based on the above analysis, you could evaluate:
> - the best way of managing cash flow
> - the most likely causes of cash-flow problems
> - the optimum solutions for cash-flow problems
> - the interrelationships between the above three factors
> - conclusions that could be drawn from the data

Measuring and increasing profit

Distinction between cash and profit

Cash is money coming into the business in the form of sales revenue. However, not all that cash will turn into profit, as a business has to pay for the cost of sales (including raw materials and labour production costs) and other overheads (including rent and rates, marketing, salaries, heating and lighting etc.).

So, sales revenue – cost = profit (net profit)

In the short term, positive cash flow is the most important factor. A business can look very profitable on paper, with full order books, but until that money is received the liquidity of the business may be threatened, e.g. if the business has to pay suppliers for raw materials up front but there are delays to receiving money for finished goods.

Net profit margins

Net profit margin expresses profit as a proportion of the level of sales (turnover).

$$\text{net profit margin} = \frac{\text{net profit}}{\text{sales (turnover)}} \times 100\%$$

If a business has £18,000 in sales, variable costs of £8,000 and fixed costs of £6,400, then the net profit will be £18,000 – (£8,000 + £6,400) = £3,600.

The net profit margin will be:

$$\frac{\text{net profit}}{\text{sales}} = \frac{3,600}{18,000} \times 100\% = 20\%$$

Whether a percentage is good or bad will require comparisons with previous years' figures or with other businesses in similar industries. For example, a lowering of the percentage may indicate that the business is having problems controlling its costs, while an increase may indicate the business is becoming more efficient in controlling costs or is able to set a higher price.

Return on capital

Capital is the money put into a business by the owner(s) when it is first established, or in order to buy new equipment or machinery, or to invest in a new project. It is important that this capital brings in a suitable return for the business. Return on capital means the percentage return on this capital investment.

If a business invests £10,000 in a new project and receives a return of £500, the return on capital will be:

$$\frac{\text{return}}{\text{capital invested}} = \frac{500}{10,000} \times 100\% = 5\%$$

A return of £2,500 on the same project would be a percentage return of:

$$\frac{2,500}{10,000} \times 100\% = 25\%$$

Whether a return is good or bad may depend upon the opportunity cost. For example, a business may consider a return of 5% as too low, as it could have got 5% from the bank.

Improving profits/profitability

There are many methods a business can utilise to try to improve profitability. These could include:
- increasing prices, to widen the profit margin
- decreasing costs by:
  - sourcing cheaper supplies
  - employing fewer people
  - outsourcing production to a country with cheaper labour costs
  - reducing other costs, e.g. cutting back on advertising

Analysis This can involve:
- Assessing how a particular change might influence the figures. For example, increasing prices could lead to a decrease in demand, depending on whether demand for the product is price sensitive. This might erode any increase in profit margin.
- Analysing situations in which a higher price might have little impact on demand and so lead to much higher profits.

- Integrating the impact of price changes with an understanding of price elasticity of demand (see pp. 51–52)
- Decreasing costs by changing suppliers could lead to poorer quality of materials, with a consequent reduction in sales and hence profits as the business loses its reputation for high quality. Similarly, other methods of cost cutting may lead to lower demand or internal difficulties.

Evaluation   In order to evaluate you could:
- Question what the business could afford to do. For example, outsourcing production can incur short-term costs in terms of redundancies and expense of searching for a suitable supplier.
- Look at the short-term versus the long-term implications of these proposals. For example, although cutting back on advertising can save costs in the short term, the business could lose sales leading to lower profitability in the long term.
- Draw upon information in the text in order to judge the merits of proposals aimed to increase profit.
- Consider the context of the particular business in the question before judging the relevant strengths of the suggested proposals.
- Make a judgement on the best way for a particular business to boost its profitability.

People in business

Improving organisational structures

Organisational structure and how it affects business performance

Traditionally, businesses are structured according to business functions such as marketing and production. This is known as functional management.

Functional management

Jobs are grouped together and organised into departments, sections or functions, e.g. Marketing, Finance, Production. This form of management can lead to:
- clearly defined channels of communication and hierarchy
- clearly defined roles
- decision making being more centralised

In order to build more flexibility into the structure of the organisation, matrix management is often introduced.

Organisational hierarchies and structures are useful to define accountability and to clarify roles, but they discourage flexibility and can become quickly outdated. Spans of control and hierarchies are closely linked — the *wider* the span of control the *fewer* the levels in the hierarchy.

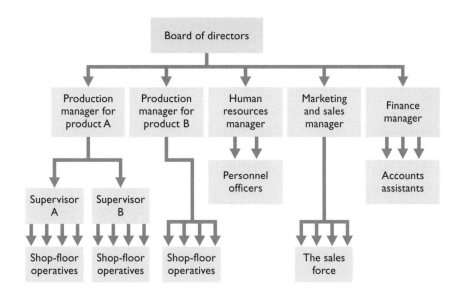

Levels of hierarchy

Levels of hierarchy means the number of levels of management within an organisation. A company that has many levels of hierarchy will have a tall organisational structure, whereas one with fewer levels of hierarchy will have a flatter organisational structure.

Many levels in the hierarchy (tall structure)

The pros and cons of this kind of structure are as follows:

- greater opportunities for specialisation
- greater opportunities for promotion
- can create communication problems between the top and the bottom of the organisation when there are many layers through which communication has to pass
- organisational culture may be more bureaucratic
- may be less opportunity for delegation
- administration costs may be higher

Few levels in the hierarchy (flat structure)

A flatter structure has the characteristics listed below:

- fewer opportunities for specialisation
- fewer opportunities for promotion
- communication between top and bottom of the hierarchy is easier as there are fewer levels to pass through
- may be greater opportunities for delegation
- administration costs may be lower

Wide versus narrow span of control

Wide span of control

A wide span means that:

- there will be greater opportunities for delegation
- supervision and control will be looser
- the distance between the top and the bottom of the organisation will be smaller
- there is reduced contact and communication between managers and reportees
- if accompanied by delayering (removal of a level of hierarchy), this can lead to lower costs but also reduced opportunities for promotion

Narrow span of control

In a narrow span:

- there is less opportunity for delegation
- supervision and control are tighter
- distance between the top and bottom of the organisation is greater
- there is greater contact between managers and reportees
- possibly greater opportunities for promotion exist

The span of control can depend on:

- the expertise of the manager and his/her ability to control a larger number of people and delegate tasks effectively
- the motivation of employees and their ability to work on their own with little supervision
- the complexity of the task — complex tasks may require a narrow span and closer supervision depending on the skill level of the workforce

Centralised versus decentralised structures

Centralisation involves authority and responsibility for decision making being in the hands of senior managers. Decentralisation means that this responsibility is given to individual units, departments, branches or lower-level managers.

Centralised decision making may result in:

- greater control over decisions made
- more consistency
- more efficient use of specialist skills of employees and managers

Decentralised decision making may result in:

- increased motivation due to the empowerment of lower-level managers
- the development of skills in lower-level managers
- quicker decision making — but it will be difficult for these lower-level managers to have an overview and be aware of the wider impact of their decisions

Workforce roles

Workforce roles will depend upon the size of the organisation and type of business. When a business is first starting out, employees may have to undertake many different roles, e.g. manager of employees, sales and finance (a jack of all trades). As the business expands, there are greater opportunities to specialise and employ additional staff for these roles. The levels in the hierarchy will increase and the workforce roles will become more specific, e.g. instead of one person fulfilling many functions there will be a personnel manager, sales manager and financial manager. The organisational structure will evolve with the creation of further workforce roles, ranging from directors at the top of the organisation to managers of departments, team leaders in those departments, supervisors and operatives.

The roles of these jobs are summarised below:
- The managing **director** assumes overall leadership of the company. He or she delegates responsibility for functional areas such as production and finance to managers who are employees of the business.
- The **manager** has, as the title suggests, responsibility for a functional area of the business, such as marketing. He or she will be responsible for the team leaders.
- The **team leader** coordinates the work of a particular part of the functional area/department. For example, in marketing there may be team leaders responsible for the marketing of individual products or activities such as merchandising and market research.
- In large departments, with many members in a team, there may need to be **supervisors**. These are the line managers who liaise with team leaders in order to guide the **operatives**.
- The **operatives** are the main body of employees in a department. For example, in a production department they would make the products.

Delegation

Tasks are handed down by a manager to a subordinate. The subordinate is given the authority to make decisions but the manager remains accountable. The process can be a way of motivating and empowering employees.

For delegation to be effective the manager must:
- think carefully about getting the right person to do the job
- ensure he or she is adequately trained
- ensure that the interesting tasks, as well as more boring ones, are delegated
- provide support mechanisms

Communication flows and consultation

Communication flows in an organisation are shown by the organisation chart.

Vertical communication takes place between a manager and a subordinate (e.g. a director and a manager).

Horizontal communication takes place between two individuals at the same level of the hierarchy (e.g. between the human resources director and the finance director or between two operatives working in the same team).

Although vertical communication down the line, from a manager to a subordinate, is arguably the most common form of communication, more democratic organisations will encourage upward (bottom-up) forms of communication. This process arises from consultation.

Consultation involves asking employees about their views on various issues. These views may then be taken into account before decisions are made. However, ultimately the decisions are made by the manager. (This links in with motivation theories such as Herzberg.)

Analysis Consider the advantages and disadvantages of the different structures and features of organisations. Link these positive and negative factors to the circumstances of a scenario given. Examples include:
- centralised structure versus decentralised structure in a particular situation
- reasons for/weaknesses of hierarchical structure
- narrow versus wide span of control
- causes/consequences of delayering
- reasons for functional management
- implications of changes in management structure

Evaluation Opportunities for evaluation in this area include:
- recognising that structures can be influenced by the size and type of organisation, culture, attitudes of owners and senior managers etc.
- acknowledging that attitudes to structural changes will depend on whether they are brought about for positive or negative reasons and how they are 'sold' to employees
- recognising the capability of organisations to evolve and develop and be able to adapt, particularly in dynamic environments

Links A basic requirement of the AS course is to integrate elements of the specification wherever possible. Below are a few examples of how to link organisational structures with other areas of human resource management.

Organisations with wider spans of control can give greater opportunities for job enlargement and enrichment and empowering of employees. Alternatively, if communication systems are poor it could lead to motivational problems. If a wider span of control is achieved by delayering, employees may fear for their job security, causing motivational problems (Herzberg's hygiene factors; Maslow's security needs). Decentralised structures should increase the motivation levels of employees. Matrix structures are also associated with higher levels of motivation than traditional functional structures.

Delegation can be an opportunity to empower employees and increase their motivation (Herzberg's motivators; Maslow's higher level needs). Whether it does motivate will depend upon the way in which the tasks are delegated and the culture of the organisation. With consultation, employees will feel involved in the decision-making process, but is the consultation real or just 'lip service'?

Widening or narrowing the span of control will have implications for recruitment, selection and training. Employees will need training to take on the extra role responsibilities. Delayering will result in job losses either through natural wastage, redeployment or redundancies.

Delegation again may have implications for training existing employees, depending on the extent of the proposed delegation. Managers also need to ensure that new employees have the necessary skills to take on additional responsibility.

Measuring the effectiveness of the workforce

Labour productivity

Labour productivity can be calculated using the following formula:

$$\text{labour productivity} = \frac{\text{output}}{\text{number of employees}}$$

If the output of a factory is 80,000 units per year and it employs 200 employees,

$$\text{labour productivity} = \frac{80,000}{200} = 400 \text{ units per employee}$$

Labour turnover

Labour turnover is calculated as a percentage, as follows:

$$\text{labour turnover} = \frac{\text{number of staff leaving per year}}{\text{average number of staff employed per year}} \times 100$$

So, if a firm employs 450 employees and 36 employees leave in a year:

$$\text{labour turnover} = \frac{36}{450} \times 100 = 8\%$$

Analysis This can involve considering:
- a comparison of the figures with those of previous years to see whether they have improved or worsened (NB a decreasing labour turnover figure is an improvement)
- the implications of improvement in labour productivity (e.g. reduction in costs per unit which could lead to better profitability for the business)
- reasons why productivity has improved (e.g. is it due to introduction of new equipment or machinery, or has motivation improved leading to higher output?)
- reasons for deterioration in labour turnover (e.g. are terms and conditions of employment poor? Are motivation levels low?)

Evaluation In order to evaluate, you could:

- consider the long-term implications for the business of high levels of labour turnover (e.g. in terms of impact on morale or image of the organisation)
- recognise that increased labour productivity on its own will not improve profitability unless accompanied by other factors such as efficient marketing and a good quality product

Developing an effective workforce: recruitment, selection, training

Recruitment and selection process

This is the process by which an organisation fulfils its need to find new employees. It requires the organisation to address the following questions:

- What is the job that needs to be filled? (job description)
- Are there any alternatives available? (redeployment, increased overtime, temporary agency staff, new technology, outsourcing, insourcing)
- Does the organisation deal with the recruitment process or does it use an agency or a consultant?
- What does the job entail? (job description)
- What type of person is needed to fill the vacancy? (person specification)
- How can the organisation attract sufficient numbers of suitable applicants to apply? (which advertising media should it use?)
- How do applicants apply for the job? (application form, curriculum vitae, letter of application)
- How can the organisation decide if the applicants are suitable? (interview, psychometric testing, assessment centres)
- What are the legal implications? (Sex Discrimination Act, Race Relations Act, Disability Discrimination Act, Employment (Equality) Age Regulations)

The method of recruitment and selection used depends on:

- level of job within the organisation
- location of the job
- size of the organisation
- resources available
- cost
- supply of labour
- historical factors
- approach and attitudes of management

Internal or external recruitment?

Internal recruitment is recruiting an employee from within the organisation.

Advantages:

- Advertising is cheap, e.g. via intranet, notice board, newsletter.
- The applicant already knows the organisation, potentially reducing costs of induction training.
- The applicant is known in terms of his or her potential for the post.
- It can create promotional opportunities, potentially increasing motivation among staff.

Disadvantages:

- New ideas or a fresh approach may not be generated.
- There will be a limited source of potential applicants, if only this method is used.
- It may create a vacancy elsewhere in the organisation which will need to be filled; recruitment costs may consequently increase rather than decrease.

External recruitment is recruiting an employee from outside the organisation.

Advantages:

- Applicants may bring in new ideas or fresh approaches to the organisation.
- There is a wider pool of applicants to choose from.

Disadvantages:

- It is more expensive.
- The process will take longer.
- The applicant is not known to the organisation and does not have a proven record.

Analysis Opportunities for analysis include:

- matching up the method of recruitment and selection with the needs of the particular organisation
- looking at why methods vary according to the level of job and expertise required
- considering whether the methods being used by the organisation under consideration are the most appropriate
- considering the costs versus benefits of the elements involved in the recruitment and selection process

Evaluation Opportunities for evaluation include:

- considering whether a recruitment process is planned systematically or is unplanned and unsystematic
- considering the impact of effective recruitment and selection — this is difficult to measure but it could lead to lower labour turnover, lower costs and more highly motivated employees
- evaluation of how well a particular recruitment process was organised

Links There are close links to other human resource topics such as training and motivation theories. Other factors such as training, wages offered and working conditions can affect the availability of labour and therefore the recruitment and selection methods that will be used.

Training

Training is the process that attempts to fill the gap between what the employee has already in terms of accumulated skills, knowledge and attributes and what is demanded by the job now and possibly in the future. This can be part of:

- induction
- training for change
- training for personal development
- skills development
- team building
- attitude training

A range of methods can be used, involving:

- in-house or external training or a mixture of both
- on-the-job or off-the-job training
- courses
- mentoring
- coaching
- work shadowing
- personalised study programmes
- open-learning packages

Decisions regarding methods to be used should be taken after identifying training needs. Examples of how this process could be conducted are:

- training needs analysis
- staff appraisal
- assessment centres

Ideally, the training provision that is best for a particular individual and the organisation should be chosen, but cost is often the biggest determining factor.

Internal or external training?

Internal training takes place within the organisation in a work context. It is appropriate if training needs are specific to the individual organisation. Internal training that makes use of internal trainers and external providers can lead to the best of both worlds. The most common form of internal training is on-the-job training.

External training takes place away from the workplace. It is appropriate if there are only a few employees with this specific training need and the training requirement is not specifically linked to the organisation. It gives trainees the opportunity to meet people from other organisations, allowing for an interchange of ideas and a broadening of understanding. This can also make employees feel valued and increase their motivation.

On-the-job or off-the-job training?

On-the-job training (sitting next to Nellie) is likely to:
- be cheaper, as existing employees and equipment can be used
- take place in a realistic environment so there should be no problems in readjusting from a learning to a work situation

However, problems may result from:
- the employee conducting the training being a poor instructor who is unable to teach the proper skills
- the employee conducting the training having developed bad habits/short cuts that are passed on to the trainee
- the work situation being noisy and stressful and not the best learning environment

Off-the-job training often uses specially trained experts to provide the training. This approach may result in:
- training being more highly valued by employees, leading to increased motivation
- opportunities to meet staff from other organisations and learn about their systems
- reduced stresses and distractions, because of being away from the workplace

Purpose and benefits of training

- ensures the employee has the necessary skills, knowledge and attributes required for the job
- can identify potential for the future
- increases efficiency
- reduces costs in the long term
- can lead to increased motivation
- increases employees' job prospects

Analysis Opportunities for analysis include considering:
- the cost versus benefits of training
- relevance of the training provision in the context of a given organisation
  - is it needs driven or imposed?
  - is it training for the sake of it or does it provide valuable benefits to all concerned?

Evaluation Training has an important influence upon the success of a business. Many organisations adopt a short-term approach to training, seeing it as an unnecessary cost and one that can be easily cut. They fail to weigh up the long-term advantages to the organisation and the individual. The importance of training and how it is perceived by the organisation and the employees will greatly influence its success.

Links There are possible links with motivation and other human resource issues. External and internal change of any nature may often give rise to training needs.

Developing and retaining an effective workforce: motivating employees

Motivation is an internal psychological process which is self-initiated and influenced by culture, family and social values, and the actions of other people.

Motivation theory

There are many theories of motivation. Familiarity with the theories of Maslow, Herzberg, Mayo and Taylor should give you a broad range of ideas that can be applied to the scenarios in the examination papers.

Maslow

According to Maslow, human needs consist of five types which form his **hierarchy of needs**. Starting from the most basic needs, they are as follows:

(1) Physiological — good wage and salary structure, good working conditions.
(2) Safety — security at work (a safe job), pension arrangements, safe working environment.
(3) Social — opportunities for teamworking, social events.
(4) Esteem — providing positive feedback where possible and chances for promotion.
(5) Self-actualisation — providing challenging new tasks and roles within the organisation.

Herzberg

Herzberg divided the factors motivating people at work into two groups:

(1) Hygiene factors — salary, security, supervision, working conditions, company policy. Improvements to these might remove dissatisfaction, but they will not increase satisfaction and motivation.
(2) Motivators — recognition, responsibility, work itself, achievement, advancement. Improvements in these areas will lead to increases in motivation.

Mayo

Mayo's research led him to draw the following conclusions:

- Employees are motivated by more than money and working conditions.
- Work is a group activity and employees should be seen as members of a group.
- Recognition, belonging and security are more important in influencing motivation than working conditions.
- Informal groups exert an important influence over employees' attitudes.
- Supervisors need to pay attention to individuals' social needs and the influence of informal groups.

Taylor

Taylor regarded the worker as an 'economic animal responding directly to financial incentives' (the 'rational economic man'). He invented work study and founded the scientific approach to management, which aimed at maximising efficiency through specialisation. Although highly influential during the twentieth century, his methods meant that jobs became boring and repetitive. He believed that workers are motivated by money and try to avoid work, so they need close supervision.

Motivation in practice

Why is motivation important?

Poor morale in an organisation can lead to:

- high levels of absenteeism
- high levels of labour turnover
- higher costs for the organisation due to the above factors
- poor image, which could cause problems in recruiting and retaining employees
- lower productivity
- loss of competitive advantage

A number of different methods have been tried and tested to improve morale and motivation based on the various motivation theories, including **improving job design**, **empowerment**, **teamworking** and **financial incentives**.

Improving job design

This may take the form of:

- job enrichment
- job enlargement

Job enrichment

This is a means of giving employees greater responsibility and offering them challenges that allow them to utilise their skills fully.

The advantages of job enrichment are as follows:

- It develops workers' skills and presents them with challenges.
- It allows workers to make greater contributions to the decision-making process.
- It enhances workers' promotional prospects.
- It motivates workers by ensuring that their abilities and potential are exploited and that individuals gain a high degree of self-control over the setting of goals and the identification of how to achieve those goals.

The disadvantages of job enrichment are as follows:

- Some workers may feel that it places additional pressure on them that they do not want.
- It could be seen simply as a way to delegate responsibility down through the hierarchy and to reduce the number of employees by delayering.
- Not all jobs lend themselves to enrichment. For example, routine production line work may give little scope for greater responsibility.

Job enlargement

This involves increasing the scope of a job, either by job enrichment or by job rotation, where a worker takes a variety of roles, usually at the same level of responsibility.

The advantages of job enlargement are as follows:
- It motivates workers through giving them greater recognition, improving their promotion prospects and increasing the feelings of achievement arising from the job itself.
- It can relieve the boredom of the work.
- If a person is absent, others can cover the job without difficulty.
- Workers may be more motivated because of their wider range of skills and they will become more flexible.
- There may be a greater sense of participation in the production process.

The disadvantages of job enlargement are as follows:
- A firm can demoralise its workforce by giving them excessive workloads.
- Retraining costs will increase and there may be a fall in output because there is less specialisation.
- It could be seen as simply involving a greater number of boring tasks but with a reduction in the social benefits of working, since groups will be constantly changing.

Empowerment

This can be achieved through informal systems or through formal structures, such as autonomous work groups, giving employees autonomy and decision-making powers. The aim is to increase motivation while also improving flexibility and quality, thus adding value to the organisation.

Teamworking

When accompanied by other techniques such as job rotation, enrichment and some degree of decision making, teamworking can enhance motivation and/or relieve the boredom of a monotonous job. This ties in with Mayo's principles and Maslow's social needs.

Financial incentives

These range from piece rates to profit sharing and share-ownership schemes. Links can be made with Taylor's view of 'rational economic man', Maslow's physiological needs and Herzberg's hygiene factors.

Analysis Opportunities for analysis in this area include:
- Linking motivational theories into a scenario to highlight issues raised.
- Looking critically at the theories in the context of a situation being considered.
- Recognising that introducing motivational techniques does not necessarily lead to increased productivity.
  For example. It may just mean that people are happier doing their jobs and are more receptive to change. Remember it is not just work factors that can motivate people. Employees may get their higher-level needs satisfied outside the working environment and just want the money.

Evaluation Opportunities for evaluation in this area include:
- acknowledging that everyone is different and that theories may need to be adjusted to the conditions

- recognising that motivational factors will change over time and are not static
- realising that past experiences may influence an individual's motivation
- emphasising that while theories are useful as a starting-point, organisations should never lose sight of the fact that motivation is a complex issue

Links This topic has links with most of the areas in this module. Whenever people issues are at the forefront, motivation and what 'makes people tick' will be important factors to be considered. However, avoid making reference to motivation and theorists' viewpoints at every possible opportunity. While motivation may be a relevant factor in many areas, care should be taken to ensure that a wider perspective is shown and that the actual question being asked is addressed.

Operations management
Making operational decisions

Operational targets

These may be set in terms of:
- Improvement in unit costs — measured by a reduction in costs, potentially leading to increased profits.
- Improvement in quality — measured by a reduction in wastage, decrease in level of complaints etc.
- Increased capacity utilisation — measured by an increase in actual output as a percentage of maximum possible output.

Unit costs

The unit cost is the cost of producing one unit of output. It is calculated by the following formula:

$$\frac{\text{total cost}}{\text{units of output}} = \text{unit cost}$$

The unit cost is also known as the average cost (AC) or average total cost (ATC).

For example, ABC Ltd produces 40 units of output at a total cost of £60. Its average (or unit) cost is:

$$\frac{£60}{40} = £1.50$$

In order to measure efficiency, ABC Ltd can compare its unit costs with those of its competitors. The business with the lowest unit costs will be the most efficient, in terms of this particular measure.

Unit costs of four different companies

	Units of output	Total costs (£)	Unit costs (£)
ABC Ltd	40	60	1.50
DEF Ltd	30	57	1.90
GHI Ltd	100	1,650	1.65
JKL Ltd	120	1,740	1.45

ABC Ltd is the second most efficient company as JKL Ltd's unit costs are slightly lower.

Analysis Opportunities for analysis include:
- looking at the key factors that influence a firm's unit costs
- comparing ways of improving (lowering) unit costs
- analysing the implications of data on unit costs, in terms of factors that have caused high/low costs and the implications of these costs

Measuring quality

It should be recognised that firms will use different measures of quality according to the needs of the firm or its customers. Examples of quality measures include:
- Customer satisfaction ratings — a survey of customers can reveal customer opinions on a numerical scale (e.g. 1 to 10).
- Customer complaints — this calculates the number of customers who complain (it is sometimes measured as a percentage of the total number of customers).
- Scrap rate (%) — this calculates the number of items rejected during the production process as a percentage of the number of units produced.
- Punctuality — this calculates the degree to which a business delivers its products (or provides its services) on time. It is often measured as a percentage:

$$\frac{\text{deliveries on time}}{\text{total deliveries}} \times 100 = \text{punctuality}$$

Analysis Opportunities for analysis include:
- interpreting the meaning of a statistical measure of quality in terms of whether it is showing high or poor quality
- comparing changes in quality between different organisations or over time
- selecting and explaining the best ways of measuring quality in a particular situation

Calculating and managing capacity utilisation

Capacity utilisation measures the percentage of a firm's total possible production level that is being reached at present. It is calculated as follows:

$$\frac{\text{actual output per annum}}{\text{maximum possible output per annum}} \times 100 = \text{capacity utilisation (\%)}$$

It can also be measured over any chosen time period. For many organisations it may be more appropriate to calculate it on a daily, weekly or monthly basis.

There is no one ideal target percentage, but many people believe that 90% capacity utilisation is a sensible level. At 100% there is no scope for maintenance and repair or to deal with emergency situations that may occur. However, every percentage point below 100 represents 'unused' resources and higher fixed costs.

Spare capacity (or under-utilisation) measures the extent to which production falls below the maximum possible level. Thus, a company on 90% capacity utilisation has a spare capacity of 10%.

Possible causes of under-utilisation include:
- new competitors or new products entering the market
- fall in demand for the product as a whole due to changes in taste or fashion
- unsuccessful marketing
- seasonal demand
- over-investment in fixed assets
- a merger leading to duplication of many resources and sites (e.g. between two banks)

Possible impacts of under-utilisation include:
- a higher proportion of fixed costs per unit
- lower profit levels or the need to increase price to maintain the same levels
- a negative image and the perception that the company is unsuccessful
- employee boredom
- more time for maintenance of machinery, training, improving existing systems etc.
- less stress for employees, unless utilisation is so low that they fear for their jobs
- the ability to cater for a sudden increase in demand
- motivational issues, either positive or negative

Ways of increasing capacity utilisation are to:
- Stimulate demand for the product (link these ideas with marketing strategies and the marketing mix).
- Rationalise production (in other words, improve efficiency by reducing the scale of operations). A firm can achieve this by:
  - leasing or selling off part of the production area
  - moving towards a shorter working week or shorter day
  - laying off workers or reducing their hours

Analysis Opportunities for analysis include:
- Investigating the reasons for the under-utilisation (or over-utilisation).
- Investigating the consequences of the under-utilisation (or over-utilisation).
- Suggesting ways of solving the problem of under-utilisation (or over-utilisation).
- Looking at the implications of operating at full capacity or under-utilising capacity in the context of the particular organisation being studied. Either option can be positive

or negative, depending on the circumstances of the organisation. Link in your answer to real-life examples where possible.

Evaluation Opportunities for evaluation include considering whether under-utilisation is a deliberate choice made for positive reasons or one the organisation has been forced into due to external factors, such as decreased demand. The benefits of under-utilisation, e.g. more time being devoted to training and improving existing systems, are more likely to be experienced if it is a positive choice. If forced into under-utilisation the impact is more likely to be negative, as the focus may well be less on long-term growth and more on short-term survival. The negative impact on morale and motivation is also likely to be a major factor.

When looking at ways of increasing utilisation again, differentiation is needed between short- and long-term solutions. In the short term, an organisation is more likely to reduce hours and move to a shorter working week. In the long term, redundancies and selling off production units may be the only solution. Ways of stimulating demand can fit into either short- or long-term categories.

Links There are links too with marketing strategies where firms are trying to stimulate demand. An understanding of costs and profit is also required — unused resources will affect profitability in the short term, but may be needed for long-term growth.

Links to motivation Under-utilisation may lead to boredom and decreased motivation levels or it can mean less stress and increased morale — it depends on the circumstances. The organisation may have to rationalise to increase utilisation, and redundancies affect security. (Links with Herzberg's hygiene factors; Maslow's safety needs.)

Links to human resource management Reduced capacity utilisation may give the opportunity for training to take place. Needs can be identified and training put in place to meet those needs. Alternatively, in the long term, there may be the need for a reduction of jobs through natural wastage or redundancies.

Operational issues dealing with non-standard orders and matching production and demand

To overcome problems of temporary increases in demand, an organisation can:
- ask employees to work overtime
- hire in temporary or part-time employees
- use staff from an agency

Although these methods will increase costs in the short term, they tend to reduce the long-term costs of employing a person on a full-time contract.
- A firm may choose to outsource production by **sub-contracting** the work to another organisation. This removes the problem by passing it to someone else, although there are issues over control and quality.

- Stocks also need to be managed efficiently to ensure there are adequate supplies of raw materials to satisfy sudden surges in demand. This requires good links with suppliers.

Developing effective operations: quality

Quality: those features of a product or service that allow it to satisfy (or delight) customers.

Measures of quality include:
- appearance
- reliability
- functions (added extras)
- after-sales service
- image and brand
- exclusivity

Quality systems

Quality system: the approach used by an organisation in order to achieve quality. Most quality systems can be classified under two headings: quality control and quality assurance.

Benefits of having a quality system
- Impact on sales volume — if a product or service meets the needs of the customers, as described above, then demand for the product will increase.
- Creating a unique selling point (USP) — businesses can use the level of quality of their products or services as a unique selling point in order to increase demand.
- Impact on selling price — having a unique selling point created by quality allows a business to charge a higher price.
- Pricing flexibility — a reputation for quality gives a firm the ability to be more flexible in its pricing in order to target different market segments.
- Cost reductions — a quality system can reduce costs by improving production methods and reducing waste and the number of faulty products.
- The firm's reputation — a good quality system can prevent problems and help a business to avoid any damage to its reputation.

Issues involved in introducing and managing a quality system
Although the introduction of a quality system provides the benefits shown above, there are also issues and problems involved.
- Costs — quality procedures require a great deal of administrative expense to set up.
- Training — the training needed may be quite extensive and costly.
- Disruption to production — in the short run the training programme provided can be quite disruptive to existing production methods.

Quality control (inspection) versus quality assurance (self-checking)

The benefits of quality control (inspection) are:

- As inspection is at the end of the production process, it can prevent a defective product reaching the customer — thus eliminating a problem with a whole batch of product.
- It is more secure than a system that relies on one individual.
- It may detect common problems throughout the organisation.

The benefits of quality assurance (self-checking) include:

- Ownership of product rests with production operatives rather than with an independent inspector.
- It can have a positive effect on motivation, due to this sense of ownership.
- There is less need for reworking faulty products.
- There is better quality first time. This results in less waste/scrap.
- It provides cost savings.
- It helps to ensure consistent product quality.

The main method of quality assurance

Total quality management occurs where there is a culture of quality throughout the organisation. It is based on the philosophy of 'right first time'. If the individual making the product ensures quality, then there is no need for inspection.

Quality standards

ISO 9001 is a national/international quality standard. To achieve it, firms must show that they have quality systems that cover the quality of their working methods, services and processes as well as the quality of their products. The focus is on prevention (or rapid detection) of defects, ensuring that adequate support systems are in place and good teamworking exists.

The benefits of this award are:

- marketing advantages from the acknowledgement of higher quality standards
- assurance to customers that products meet certain standards — some organisations insist on these awards before agreeing to trade with a firm, as this helps to guarantee the quality of their supplies
- greater employee motivation from the sense of responsibility and recognition
- financial benefits in the long term, from the elimination of waste and the improved reputation of the firm

Analysis Opportunities for analysis include:

- assessing the costs of poor quality in terms of scrap, rework, increased inspection costs and poor image, as opposed to the costs of achieving a first-class product

- recognising that prevention is the key to total quality, from the supplier right through to the customer, and that this cannot take place without adequate support and commitment from everyone within an organisation
- pointing out that teams need to be empowered with authority to stop the production process whenever a defect is discovered
- considering the advantages and disadvantages of introducing a quality system and/or the problems in setting it up

Evaluation Opportunities for evaluation include:
- Recognising that quality has become one of the most important factors in staying ahead of the competition. Traditionally, British companies have not always focused on what the customer wants and this may be one reason for their lack of competitive advantage over, for example, Japanese producers.
- Underlining that the identification and satisfaction of customers' needs should be given top priority by organisations if they wish to retain their competitive edge. Quality is subjective and firms should tailor their approach to the customers' needs.
- Pointing out that companies considering whether to take corrective action should also consider the likely responses of their competitors.

Links There are links to marketing — to achieve a competitive advantage based on the points examined above, organisations need to become more focused on customer needs. This requires extensive market research and constant feedback and development of new products.

Developing effective operations: customer service

Methods of meeting customer expectations

Customer service is concerned with ensuring that the needs of every single customer are met. Customer expectations can be met by:
- Ensuring the organisation is selling what the customer wants. This can be monitored by undertaking market research.
- Ensuring that the product or service sold is of high quality.
- Ensuring that staff are friendly, helpful and knowledgeable about the product/service being offered.
- Ensuring that staff are efficient in dealing with customers.
- Ensuring that genuine customer complaints are dealt with efficiently and courteously.

If someone has a good customer experience, they will tell a handful of people. If they have a bad experience, they will tell everyone they know.

Monitoring and improving customer service

Methods of monitoring and improving customer service include:
- Setting up systems for customer feedback, customer surveys and suggestion boxes to assess customer satisfaction. Using focus groups, mystery shoppers or observation methods to monitor employees' customer service skills and knowledge of product/service.
- Ensuring improvements are made in the light of comments and information received as part of the monitoring process.
- Training employees to ensure product/service knowledge and customer service skills.

Benefits of high levels of customer service

Benefits to an organisation of high levels of customer service include:
- customers return
- it gains competitive advantage
- it creates a USP
- it creates a good image for the organisation
- it ensures long-term viability of the business

> **Analysis** Opportunities for analysis include:
> - assessing the cost of training, having better quality materials etc. against the cost of loss of customers
> - considering the advantages of monitoring and improving customer service

> **Evaluation** Opportunities for evaluation include:
> - Recognising that customers have different perceptions about what constitutes good customer service. Some are more concerned about the quality of the product/service; others are more interested in the whole customer experience.
> - Recognising that some customers are concerned with receiving value for money, which doesn't necessarily mean that the product or service is cheap but that the customer is satisfied that the product/service is worth the money they have paid.
> - Recognising the short-term cost of getting it right first time against the long-term cost to the business of loss of customers and falling profit levels.
> - Recognising that training employees to provide excellent customer service is just the start of the process. It is important to monitor, assess and evaluate customer service constantly to ensure the organisation meets and exceeds customer demands.

Working with suppliers

Choosing effective suppliers

Many factors will affect an organisation's choice of supplier:
- Price of raw materials — important if it is to make a sufficient level of profit.

- Quality of raw materials — to ensure the end product also has good quality.
- Trade credit terms — favourable terms may enable an organisation to delay payments and improve cash flow.
- Reliability of supplier — they must be able to satisfy demands efficiently.
- Length of lead times — to ensure production is not held up.
- Flexibility of supplier — they may need to be able to satisfy sudden increases in demand.

Role of suppliers in improving operational performance

Suppliers play an important role in improving operational performance. They do this by ensuring that the right raw materials of the best quality at the optimum price are available to the organisation in time for it to fulfil its customers' orders.

Analysis Opportunities for analysis include:
- assessing the importance of the supplier in the context of the organisation
- considering the advantages and disadvantages of an effective/ineffective supplier

Evaluation Opportunities for evaluation include:
- recognising there is a trade off between low price of raw materials and quality
- considering and weighing up the factors affecting choice of suppliers in terms of their importance to this organisation
- considering the effectiveness of suppliers in terms of stock control and their ability to react quickly and be flexible when needed

Using technology in operations

Types of technology in operations management

The AQA specification highlights the following four examples of technology in operations management:
- **Robotics** are used in many production situations, e.g. in the production of the Mini, the body-building process is highly automated with the use of robotics.
- **Automated stock control** enables accurate records to be kept of stock levels of raw materials and finished goods. Automatic reordering can take place as part of this process, ensuring greater efficiency.
- **Communications** methods can involve any or all of intranet, internet, e-mail, teleconferencing etc. These speed up communication processes and enable communication with different sections or organisations to be more efficient.
- **Design technology** involves using computer aided design (CAD), which enables designs of new products to be produced and modified on screen in three-dimensional format.

Issues in introducing and updating technology

The benefits of technology are as follows:
- Technology replaces labour and therefore reduces labour costs.
- It brings improvements in quality, as organisations are more likely to get it right first time.
- It reduces waste, for the same reason.
- It increases productivity and therefore reduces the costs of production.
- It makes monitoring stock levels much easier.
- It ensures that stock is automatically reordered, removing human error.
- It makes for ease of communication.
- It makes it easier to update product design.

The drawbacks of technology are as follows:
- The initial costs of investing in new technology will be high.
- Technology will constantly have to be updated, costing money.
- Employees will need to be trained in the use of new technology.
- Maintenance costs may be high.
- It can lead to motivation problems, if employees fear being replaced by machines.
- It can lead to information overload, e.g. employees not reading e-mails.

Analysis Opportunities for analysis include:
- assessing the importance of the technology in the context of the organisation
- considering the advantages and disadvantages of the use of technology in various business settings

Evaluation Opportunities for evaluation include:
- recognising that technology is a necessity for most businesses in some format
- recognising that although the costs may be lowered in the long term, the short-term costs will be higher due to the expense of installing new technology

Marketing and the competitive environment

Effective marketing

The Chartered Institute of Marketing defines marketing as 'the process responsible for identifying, anticipating and satisfying customer requirements profitably'.

This definition summarises the purposes of marketing, which are to:
- **Anticipate customers' wants.** The first stage of marketing is to conduct market research in order to discover the wants of customers.

- **Satisfy those requirements in a way that delights customers.** The approach used by organisations to achieve this aim is known as the marketing mix (the four Ps). An organisation will plan a suitable **product**, charge an attractive **price**, put the product into the right location or **place** and use **promotion** to make customers aware of the product.
- **Meet the needs of the organisation.** Ultimately marketing is intended to enable a business to meet its aims and objectives, such as earning profit.

Niche or mass marketing

Should the firm aim its product at a particular market segment (niche marketing), or at the whole market (mass marketing)? Both niche and mass marketing strategies can meet most of an organisation's marketing objectives. On the one hand, attracting a mass market can increase sales and thus provide security. On the other, finding the right niche ensures market positioning, and innovative products will reach new segments.

Advantages of niche marketing
- There may be fewer competitors, as large companies are not attracted to a relatively small market.
- Small firms can compete more effectively in a niche market because large firms will be less able to produce goods at low unit costs if demand is limited.
- The limited demand may suit a small firm that would lack the resources to produce on a large scale. A sole trader, for example, would only be able to produce enough products for a small market niche.
- A firm can adapt its product to meet the specific needs of the niche market, rather than compromise between the needs of many different groups of consumers.
- It can be easier for firms to target customers and promote their products effectively when they are only selling to a certain type of customer. The content of advertisements can be designed to appeal to the specific market segment being targeted.

Disadvantages of niche marketing
- The small scale of the market limits the chances of high profit.
- Small firms in niche markets can be vulnerable to changes in demand as they may have no alternative products to fall back on.
- An increase in popularity may attract larger, more efficient firms into the market.

Advantages of mass marketing
- Large-scale production is possible, which will help to lower costs per unit through factors such as bulk buying.
- The high number of customers enables companies to earn huge revenues.
- Mass marketing allows firms to use the most expensive (and usually the most effective) marketing.
- Mass markets help firms to fund the research and development costs needed to introduce new products.

- Mass marketing increases brand awareness, which can help to sell a range of products.

Disadvantages of mass marketing
- High fixed capital costs are incurred, such as the purchase of large factories. This may prevent some firms from operating in the mass market.
- Firms in mass markets may be less flexible in the face of change, such as a sudden reduction in popularity of a product.
- It can be difficult to appeal directly to each individual customer because mass-market products must be designed to suit all customers.
- There is less scope for adding value. High income customers may prefer high priced, unique products.

Consumer marketing versus business-to-business marketing

Not all marketing involves individual customers. Companies such as manufacturers will buy raw materials from other companies. Retailers will tend to buy their products directly from manufacturers. These activities are known as business-to-business transactions. Persuading a business to buy products requires different approaches to those needed when targeting individual customers. This is business-to-business (b2b) marketing.

The main features of business-to-business marketing are as follows:
- Transactions are much larger.
- Buyers and sellers have more specialist knowledge.
- The buyer's reputation often depends on the quality of the product purchased from the seller, so there may be more emphasis on this aspect.
- Promotions and advertisements tend to be more informative than persuasive, as buyers tend to base their decisions on factual information.
- Customer service is vital because poor service tends to become well known more quickly than in consumer marketing.

Designing an effective marketing mix

The success of the marketing mix depends upon ensuring that all the elements come together and are fully integrated. Many factors influence the elements of the mix. Examples include:
- Market research results may determine the price a business charges for its products/services and the places where these are sold.
- Availability of finance may influence the amount of money spent on promotion and product development.
- New technology may influence how often the product needs to be updated or whether it is made available for sale over the internet.

> **Tip** Look for ways to integrate the different elements of the four Ps. Although, for the sake of convenience, the four Ps are taught separately, the marketing mix must be integrated. Where appropriate look closely at the text in the examination to see how the different Ps need to work together. The mix will be influenced by factors such as the bullet points listed above, the market segment(s) being targeted and the actions of competitors.

Using the marketing mix: product

Product is the central feature of the marketing mix. The key elements to be understood are:

- **Design of a product.** To the consumer this means reliability, safety, convenience of use and whether it is fashionable, aesthetic and durable. To the organisation, the key elements are whether the product satisfies consumer tastes, the financial viability, its effect on reputation and whether the company can produce it without difficulty.
- **New product development.** You need to know the stages involved in introducing a new product (from initial screening to the final launch). Link new product development to the product life cycle, Boston matrix, mind showering (also known as 'brainstorming'), market research and R&D (research and development). These will be the sources of new product ideas. Organisations must be prepared to respond to the actions of competitors by developing new products and/or adapting existing products through the use of extension strategies. This will ensure that they keep market share.

Factors influencing new product development include the following.

Technology

- New technology can allow new products to be developed that are considered superior to existing products.
- Technology can lead to the development of totally new products.
- Production technology has advanced considerably, enabling organisations to produce goods and services that are more advanced and cheaper to produce.
- Businesses can more easily produce goods and services that are made to the individual specifications of the consumer.
- Technology is now allowing companies to be aware of consumer tastes.

Competitors' actions

- The introduction of a new product by a competitor may take away market share, forcing a business to respond.
- New products from competitors can give ideas for new products to a business.

Entrepreneurial skills of managers and owners

- If an entrepreneur can be the first to spot a gap in a market or think of a potentially successful idea, their business can gain 'first mover' advantage.

Other aspects of product

Unique selling points or propositions (USPs)

Marketing can add value by creating a unique selling point (USP). If a firm can improve customer awareness and goodwill through making its product different from rival products, it can increase both its sales volume and price. Customers are also less likely to stop buying the firm's product.

Product portfolio analysis

The aim here is to create a balance of products with widespread appeal. The Boston matrix is the usual way of showing this strategy.

Boston matrix

Firms aim to produce products with a high market share ('cash cows' if market growth is low, 'stars' if the market is growing quickly). They need to think carefully about retaining products with a low market share ('dogs' or 'problem children'). Dogs, however, shouldn't always be written off too lightly. Cadbury Whole Nut, for example, could be seen to be a dog because it has only a 1% share of a low-growth market (confectionery). However, this still represents almost £40 million in sales per year. **Gap analysis** can be used to investigate a product range to see if there are any market segments to which the product does not appeal; new products can be tailored to fit any gap that has been discovered.

Product life cycle

A firm should aim to have as many products in maturity as possible. To achieve this in the long term, the firm needs to have a policy of new product development so that it always has products in the introduction and growth stages, ready to bring to maturity when required.

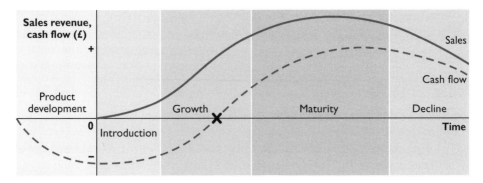

Stages in the product life cycle

In order to keep products in maturity (the most profitable stage of the product life cycle), **extension strategies** are used. Examples of extension strategies include:

- attracting new market segments
- increasing usage among existing customers
- modifying the product
- changing the image
- targeting new markets
- introducing new promotions, advertising and price offers

Using the marketing mix: promotion

Promotion attempts to draw consumers' attention to a product, brand or company. It can be above-the-line or below-the-line.

- **Above-the-line:** this is advertising through media — newspapers, television, radio, the cinema and posters.
- **Below-the-line:** this refers to all other types of promotion, such as public relations, branding, merchandising, sponsorship, direct marketing, personal selling and competitions.

Advertising can be **informative** or **persuasive**. In general, advertising aims to raise awareness, publicise changes and new products and increase brand loyalty. Other **promotions** (except public relations and sponsorship) tend to be more targeted, trying to clinch the final purchase through special offers, persuasive selling or point-of-sale displays. Companies tend to plan advertising and promotions that support each other.

The promotional mix

This consists of the various methods of promotion used in order to achieve overall marketing targets. The elements involved are as follows:

- **Public relations (PR):** PR involves gaining favourable publicity through the media.

- **Branding:** this is the process of differentiating a product or service from its competitors through the name, sign, symbol, design or slogan linked to that product.
- **Merchandising:** attempts to persuade consumers to take action at the 'point of sale'(PoS) — also known as the 'point of purchase' (PoP) — are known as merchandising. Examples include shop displays, sampling opportunities and special offers.
- **Sales promotions:** these are short-term incentives used to persuade consumers to purchase. Popular methods include competitions, free offers, coupons, 'three for the price of two' or BOGOF (buy one get one free) offers, introductory offers, product placement (featuring a product in a film), credit terms and endorsements by famous personalities.
- **Direct selling:** this takes three main forms:
  - Direct mail — promotions that are sent directly to the customer/person who has been targeted. Internet links are also used.
  - Telephone — many companies use telephone contact as it is easier to communicate directly with the customer.
  - Door-to-door drops — promotions that are delivered directly to houses. These are often delivered with the local free newspaper and can be very cost effective and targeted.
- **Personal selling:** particularly important in commercial marketing, where a company's sales force will contact other firms that are seen as potential customers.
- **Advertising:** the main media used are as follows:
  - television
  - radio
  - cinema
  - national newspapers
  - posters
  - magazines
  - internet and other electronic media
  - regional newspapers

> **Analysis** Recognise the benefits and drawbacks of each form of media and relate your responses to the circumstances in the text. Familiarise yourself with the uses of each type of media.

Influences on the choice of promotional mix

When deciding what form of promotion to choose, a business will consider the following factors:
- objectives of the campaign
- costs and budgets
- the target market
- legal factors
- customer views

Using the marketing mix: pricing

The factors that influence price are based on the forces of demand and supply. Factors influencing demand are the nature of the product, consumers' incomes, competitors' products, tastes and fashion. Supply is affected by costs of inputs (raw materials and wages mainly), technology, production methods and environmental conditions. The type of market is crucial too — the number of competitors will influence a firm's pricing, and its power to set prices will depend on its market share.

You need to know the difference between **pricing strategies** and **tactics**. There are overlaps between these classifications, but a simple distinction is outlined below.

Pricing strategies

Pricing strategies are adopted over the medium to long term to achieve marketing objectives. Such strategies include:
- **skimming pricing:** a high price set to yield a high profit margin
- **penetration pricing:** low prices set to break into a market
- **price leaders:** large companies that set market prices, which are then followed by price takers (smaller firms)
- **price takers:** small businesses that tend to follow the prices set by other firms (the price leaders)

Pricing tactics

Pricing tactics are adopted in the short term to suit particular situations. Examples of such tactics are:
- **Loss leaders:** very low prices that are used to encourage consumers to buy other, fully priced, products.
- **Psychological pricing:** prices that are set to give an impression of value (e.g. £99 rather than £100).

Influences on pricing decisions

Firms need to consider their costs when setting price, as the eventual price must be high enough to allow a reasonable level of profit for the firm. For this reason many firms use **cost-plus pricing**. This is where the firm calculates its unit costs and then adds on a *mark-up*. The mark-up allows for risk and helps the firm to make a profit by setting a price that exceeds costs.

Price elasticity of demand

Another important influence on price is the **price elasticity of demand**.

Price elasticity of demand measures how a change in the price of a good or service affects the demand for that good or service.

$$\text{price elasticity of demand} = \frac{\text{\% change in quantity demanded}}{\text{\% change in price}}$$

Note: For the AQA AS Business Studies specification, it is *not* necessary to know how to calculate the price elasticity of demand, but you do need to understand the significance of the result. For example, what is the significance of a price elasticity of demand of 0.3 in comparison to one of 2.2?

Elastic demand: if the change in price leads to a greater percentage change in the quantity demanded (ignoring the minus sign), then the calculation will yield an answer greater than 1.

Inelastic demand: if the change in price leads to a smaller percentage change in the quantity demanded, then the calculation will yield an answer less than 1.

The factors influencing the price elasticity of demand are:
- necessity
- habit
- availability of substitutes
- income of consumers
- brand loyalty

Analysis Elasticity of demand can be used to interpret the market. A brief table of data, such as the one below, can provide a lot of information.

	Product A	Product B
Price elasticity of demand	−3.5	−0.5

Conclusions for Product A
Price elasticity of demand is −3.5 (very elastic). A change in price leads to a larger change in quantity. This product is not a necessity and appears to have many close substitutes.

Conclusions for Product B
Price elasticity of demand is −0.5 (inelastic). The product is a necessity or has no close substitutes.

Marketing strategies for Product A
Short-term
- Charge a lower price to increase sales revenue, but not if the company is operating on low profit margins.

Long-term
- If profit margins are reasonable, the company may keep the price low. It may act as a cash cow, and in periods of fierce competition further price cuts should enable the company to generate high sales volumes.

Marketing strategies for Product B
Short-term
- Increase the price in order to increase the profit margin.

Long-term
- Keep the price high.
- Safeguard the product's superior image.

Evaluation In order to evaluate you could:
- Recommend an analysis of other factors/changes that influence demand.
- Point out that elasticities do not stay the same: views of products and markets can change in the short and long term.
- Look beyond the marketing implications to see the impact of price changes on operations.
- Evaluate whether recommended policies are consistent with corporate and marketing objectives.
- Discuss whether the organisation could finance the suggested strategies.

Using the marketing mix: place

This involves getting products to the places where customers can buy them. Shops do not automatically give space to suppliers. Many sales people are employed to persuade retailers to stock a product rather than trying to persuade customers to buy it. Customers cannot buy it if retailers do not sell it.

Traditionally the method of getting a product from the producer to the customer was producer > wholesaler > retailer > consumer. Many companies now bypass the wholesaler.

Think of companies/products that bypass the wholesaler. Do any bypass the retailer? Study how the internet is affecting distribution.

Factors influencing the method of distribution include:
- type of product (e.g. perishable)
- geography of the market (is it scattered?)
- complexity of the product (may need direct contact with the producer or an expert retailer)

Analysis This is an area ripe for analysis, although it is not always fruitful. Questions will require you to apply the marketing mix, and the wording of the question may require specific application (e.g. asking for a plan or method to increase sales of a particular product). Be aware that the four Ps are not equally important in all cases.
- **Product:** this is central. If it does not satisfy the customers, then the other elements cannot really overcome this. However, effective use of the other three Ps can assist success.
- **Pricing:** low prices can increase sales but this will reduce the profit margin and the firm may not be able to meet demand. Look at the circumstances in which different pricing methods or strategies can be used (e.g. when should a firm use price skimming?).

- **Promotion:** what is the most appropriate method for the product and market in question, and will it be cost effective?
- **Place:** would the firm want to keep more control of the process? Will distributors demand too much profit and will retailers stock the firm's product?

Evaluation In bold print below are two example questions. In order to evaluate, the important skill is to put yourself into the position of the firm in the question and ask: 'What decision would I take and why?'

What is the most appropriate marketing mix in a particular situation?
- **Product:** if a particular function is required (e.g. lighting), the product becomes more crucial than one that is bought for image purposes only. So what is the product? People go to a sporting event that they can watch on television — they are prepared to pay more for the 'augmented' product.
- **Pricing:** this is particularly important for products which appeal to people on low incomes. What is the price elasticity of demand?
- **Promotion:** items sold to lifestyle groups on the basis of their image rely heavily on promotion. Goods with high income elasticity can be promoted in magazines read by a particular market segment.
- **Place:** impulse buys need to be readily available and so place is vital (e.g. a minority of chocolate purchases are planned beforehand).

How much control does the company have over its marketing mix?
- **Product:** you must react to competition, expectations of customers and government legislation. People are naturally conservative and so opportunities may be less inviting than they seem at first.
- **Pricing:** unless you are a monopoly you will be limited in your scope to change price. In oligopoly (competition with a few firms) businesses try to avoid price competition, as it reduces profit margins.
- **Promotion:** your customers must be attracted to your promotions, so you will need to understand their tastes. In oligopoly, businesses use promotion as their main method of competition.
- **Place:** you must use methods that customers will accept. In practice, the retailer rather than the producer often takes this decision — it depends on the bargaining power of the two sides.

Tip As the course progresses, try to identify links between these ideas and other activities such as 'Finance', 'People' and 'Operations management'.

Marketing and competitiveness

There are a wide range of different markets providing services and products to consumers, businesses or other organisations, e.g. government departments or agencies. It will be extremely rare to be the only provider in the market. In order to compete and survive, smaller businesses will have to provide a USP, in terms of the marketing mix. This might be a more specialised product or a more convenient place to purchase it from. Even dominant businesses in the market will have to modify their marketing mixes, e.g. ensuring promotion of products perhaps in combination with alterations in prices, if they are to compete against their major competitors. Alterations of elements in the marketing mix will very often ensure success and/or survival.

Market conditions

Characteristic	Perfect competition	Monopolistic competition	Oligopoly	Monopoly
Number and size of firms	Many and small	Many and small	Few and large	One, in theory*
Nature of product	Identical	Differentiated	Differentiated	Unique
Examples	Foreign exchange market, stock market, fruit and vegetable market	Hairdressers, plumbers, cafés and insurance companies	Supermarkets, banks and motor vehicle manufacturers	Nationalised industries (pre-1980s), Royal Mail (for letters)
Barriers to entry	None; it is easy to enter or leave the market	None; it is easy to enter or leave the market	High barriers to entry	High barriers to entry
Effect on business	Price takers Cost efficiency needed for survival No real scope for marketing Very low profit margins	Some control over price Cost efficiency is important unless the firm has a strong USP Benefits from marketing Low profit	Non-price competition High overheads High profit margins but aim to achieve USP through branding High spending on promotion Collusion can occur between firms	Price setter Can become complacent Power depends on importance of the product and its alternatives High profit margins

* In theory, a monopoly is a single producer; in practice, a monopoly is defined as a firm with a market share of 25% or more.

Impact of market conditions on the marketing mix

Market conditions can affect the marketing mix. A few examples are noted below:
- Monopoly — monopolies are **price** leaders/setters and can take advantage of the lack of competition in the market in order to set very high prices. The lack of competition also means that **promotion** is not needed so much.

- Oligopoly — the **product** is vital because product differentiation is the way in which a unique selling point can be achieved. **Promotion** is important in oligopoly because it is one of the major ways in which product differentiation and unique selling points can be achieved.
- Monopolistic competition — **product** is vital in monopolistic competition, as it is the critical way in which a business can make its marketing mix different from the competition's. However, if lots of small firms are competing together there is limited opportunity for a firm to set a much lower **price** than anyone else.
- Perfect competition — because all products are identical and firms are price takers in this situation, no-one can differentiate their **prices** or **products** from anyone else's. Consequently there is also no point in **promoting** a product that cannot be distinguished from that of the competition.

Competitiveness

This is the ability of firms to sell their products successfully within the market in which they are based.

Determinants of competitiveness of a firm

Some of the key factors are listed below:

- investment in new equipment and technology
- staff skills, education and training
- innovation through investment in research and development
- enterprise
- the effectiveness of the marketing mix
- the level of staff motivation
- efficiency of operations management
- quality procedures
- the effectiveness of financial planning and control

Methods of improving competitiveness

In the light of these factors, a business can improve its competitiveness by looking at its four main functional areas and investigating ways of improving its:

- financial management
- operations management
- human resources management
- marketing

This section provides an overview of all the marketing topics. Possible lines of analysis and evaluation are listed below.

Analysis Opportunities for analysis include:

- assessing the importance of various elements of the marketing mix in the context of the organisation
- considering the advantages and disadvantages of the organisation adopting a particular strategy in terms of the marketing mix

- assessing the relative strength of the competition in the market, linking the strategies to objectives and showing how they influence each other
- considering the implications of the different stages of the product life cycle
- considering the consequences of a short (or long) product life cycle
- showing the benefits to a firm of a particular USP
- examining the implications of operating in a niche market
- comparing the merits of different extension strategies
- recognising the impact of the level of competitors/market conditions on a business

Evaluation The integrated nature of any marketing decision lends itself to evaluation. A fruitful area for both analysis and evaluation is a study of the constraints that influence marketing objectives and strategies. Opportunities for evaluation include:
- Recognising the importance of different elements of the marketing mix in consumer marketing and business-to-business marketing.
- Recognising that there are other methods of improving competitiveness apart from alterations to the marketing mix, e.g. reducing costs, improving quality, having better customer service and better trained staff. These should be linked into the context of the particular organisation.
- What are the key factors influencing the firm's competitiveness?
- Evaluate the impact of market conditions on the firm's marketing mix.

Internal constraints
- Research and development — does the company have the skills and technology to release new products?
- Finances — will marketing campaigns damage cash flow? Are sources of finance available for research and development?
- Reputation — new products can appeal to new customers and improve a firm's reputation for innovation, but a badly researched product can damage a firm's image.
- Production and operations — is the production department capable of manufacturing a new product? Will retailers stock it? Will distribution systems need to be modified? The costs of these changes should be considered.
- Other products — will the new product cannibalise (take sales from) existing company products?

External constraints
- Consumer tastes — are these known, predictable and stable, and does the product suit consumers' needs?
- Competition — how will competitors react to any changes in a firm's marketing? Will this limit the success of any strategy? How will the market conditions affect success?
- Suppliers — can they provide the organisation with the necessary materials?

Links within marketing
- Small firms may need to use niche marketing to avoid direct competition. Large markets are crucial for mass marketing, and encourage product differentiation.

- The Boston matrix links market growth and market share. The product life cycle of the product shows the scope for future growth.
- A market segment prepared to pay a premium price will help marketing to add value.
- Differentiated marketing relies on identifying market segments.
- Skilled use of promotion can increase a market (e.g. replica football shirts).
- The company with the largest market share is likely to be a price leader. Products from a price leader will gain esteem and can rely on word-of-mouth promotion.
- A decline in market share will encourage extension strategies.
- Promotions will be placed in media according to the segment that a company wishes to target.
- The market price will be higher if the product is targeted at high income groups or trend setters/early adopters.

The Sheffield College
Norton LRC
Telephone: 0114 260 2334

Questions
&
Answers

This section contains six questions, each followed by two sample answers interspersed by examiner comments.

Questions

The questions are based on the format of the AS papers. The usual pattern is for the first two or three parts of the questions to test knowledge, application and analysis building into two higher mark questions that test evaluation (the making of a reasoned judgement), in addition to the other skills.

A common problem for students (and teachers) when completing a topic is the lack of examination questions that cover only that topic. These questions have been tailored so that you can apply your learning while a topic is still fresh in your mind, either during the course or when revising in preparation for the examination.

Questions 1–4 are all focused on specific areas of the course, covered in the same order as in the Content Guidance section of this guide. These questions may be tackled during the course or on completion of the revision of that particular content area. To allow some integration and to give you more time to develop your evaluative skills, Questions 1 and 2 integrate the first two functional areas on the specification — Finance and People in business. Question 3 focuses solely on Operations management and Question 4 is based on Marketing only. Questions 5 and 6 integrate all of the topics in the Unit 2 specification and should be used for final revision purposes. The Unit 2 examination paper will consist of *two* multi-part questions worth 40 marks each. Questions 5 and 6 can be used together as a final 90-minute mock exam. In the examination you must complete two questions in 90 minutes, so allow 45 minutes to answer all parts of each question.

Sample answers

Resist the temptation to study the answers before you have attempted the questions. In each case, the first answer (by candidate A) is intended to show the type of response that would earn a grade A on that paper. An A grade does not mean perfection — these answers are intended to show the range of responses that can earn high marks. Candidate B's answers demonstrate responses that warrant a pass, but not at the A-grade level. On occasions one of the parts may include an alternative, grade A, answer. However, more often candidate B's answers will contain examples of inappropriate approaches or common mistakes. Read these answers carefully as they may help you to avoid potential problems in the examination.

Examiner comments

The examiner comments are preceded by the icon ℮. They are interspersed in the answers and indicate where credit is due. In the weaker answers, they also point out areas for improvement, specific problems and common errors, such as poor time management, lack of clarity, weak or non-existent development, irrelevance, misinterpretation of the question and mistaken meanings of terms.

Eastburys

Eastburys has been producing cider and perry for over 150 years. It is a traditional family-run business that has evolved and now incorporates a visitor centre, farm park and restaurant as part of its site. The company employs approximately 120 staff in functions ranging from marketing to distribution. The managing director has control over four directors: a personnel director, commercial director, company accountant and production director. The departments the directors lead are not of equal size.

The personnel director has two staff reporting directly to her. The commercial director manages the visitor centre, farm park and restaurant. The company accountant is in charge of the cost accountant and credit control manager, each of whom has four staff reporting directly to them.

The largest department is led by the production director. He is in charge of a technical standards manager, a distribution manager and a production manager. Under each of these managers there are four, eight and ten supervisors respectively, with anything from two to 15 employees reporting to each supervisor.

Eastburys' staff are very loyal and many have been with the company for a long time. Labour turnover is very low, except in the restaurant.

There are about 400 cider makers in the UK and the market is dominated by Bulmers of Hereford and Matthew Clark in Shepton Mallet. Both of these companies have been taken over by large multinational conglomerates and sell in excess of 90% of all cider in the UK.

Eastburys prides itself on its traditional processes, which result in the production of cider that tastes of apples rather than 'the gassy bland taste of other mass-produced ciders', according to the production director. It supplies large supermarkets with supermarket-labelled own brand cider, as well as over 30 individual Eastburys branded products to smaller retailers, pubs and restaurants. The company has recently experienced a surge in demand for cider due to the 'Magners effect': cider is becoming more fashionable as a young persons' drink, in contrast to its previous image as being for older consumers. This has resulted in an increase in demand of over 25% in the last 2 years.

At present all areas of the business are controlled financially by the company accountant. However, the board is considering allowing the restaurant to set and control its own budgets in future and become a more autonomous unit, as any profits currently are swallowed up in other areas of the business. There has also been difficulty in retaining employees in this section and sales have declined in the last few months. The restaurant is located on site in a converted milking parlour. It is fully licensed, open evenings and weekends and serves a range of high quality meals with locally sourced fresh ingredients. The staff working in the restaurant consist of a manager, a chef, two kitchen assistants and four serving staff. They have the capacity to serve 50 meals at one sitting.

In 2007 Eastburys opened a new state-of-the-art bottling plant to cope with the increased demand, at a cost of £2 million. The new facility has increased output significantly and employees received on-the-job training from other colleagues. The business borrowed £2 million from the bank at 9% interest to fund the new equipment and premises. It is anticipated that this investment will create £300,000 of profit annually for the company.

(a) Calculate the return on capital of the new bottling plant and explain whether it is financially worthwhile. (5 marks)

(b) Analyse two disadvantages of Eastburys using on-the-job training. (8 marks)

(c) To what extent will Eastburys benefit from allowing the restaurant to set its own budgets? (12 marks)

(d) Evaluate the extent to which Eastburys' organisational structure helps or hinders its performance. (15 marks)

Answer to Case Study 1: candidate A

(a) $\dfrac{300,000}{2,000,000}$ = 0.15 × 100 = 15% return

This is financially worthwhile as it is 6% higher than the 9% interest Eastburys is paying on the bank loan that it took out to pay for the new facility. However, the business should consider the risk involved. It will want to be sure that profit exceeds the £180,000 interest that it is paying on the loan.

🖉 The candidate has correctly calculated the return and explained whether it is worthwhile in the context of opportunity cost.

(b) On-the-job training is when employees are trained within the work situation, usually by another employee rather than by a qualified trainer. The disadvantages of this to the company are that the training takes place in a noisy and stressful situation, which is not always the best way for people to learn new skills as they may not hear what is being said by the instructor. In addition, those doing the training are sometimes not the best people for the job as they are not skilled trainers and are not experienced in instructing. They may assume that the other employee knows what to do and may take short cuts which could endanger safety.

🖉 The candidate has clearly explained two disadvantages of on-the-job training and developed the response in terms of the impact it could have on the business. However this has not been applied to the case study, so the candidate fails to gain application marks.

(c) If the restaurant can set its own budgets, it can assess the level of success (or failure) of its own specific activities. This information will provide the company with better direction and control to ensure that it does not overspend and that the restaurant is not subsidised by other more profitable areas of the business. The new level of autonomy can also be a motivational tool, as staff are given more authority and responsibility and gain recognition when they achieve their targets. This ties in with Herzberg's motivators, as employees will feel empowered by this recognition and their higher motivation will have positive effects on the customer experience, with people wanting to revisit the restaurant.

However, profitability may not improve if the restaurant is set unrealistic targets and this could have the opposite effect upon motivational levels. Also targets sometimes become unrealistic due to external factors, such as suppliers increasing prices causing profit levels to fall.

> 🖉 The candidate again shows sound knowledge of budgets and the advantages and disadvantages of budget setting. Good links also are made to other parts of the specification by talking about motivational theory and customer service. This leads to good analysis of points made. However, there is again no application to the case study, so the candidate again fails to pick up these marks. Although there is some judgement present, achieving higher level evaluation marks is more difficult if the answer is not contextualised.

(d) The organisational structure overall does not have many layers in the hierarchy. There are a maximum of five layers and this is only in the production area. This means that it should generally be easier to communicate ideas from the top to the bottom of the organisation. However, the organisation is a little lopsided as there are only two layers in the personnel section, compared to four in the production section. This will mean that communication is easier in some sections than others.

However, there will be difficulties in some areas as there are very wide spans of control. The greatest difficulties will be in the production area as two managers in this section have eight and ten supervisors under them. Furthermore, some of these supervisors have up to 15 employees reporting to them. This can cause difficulties in terms of communication, and supervision and control will be much looser. Both of these could affect performance, as employees may not know what to do and may not work as well if they are not being watched constantly. However, if the tasks being undertaken are not very complex, there is often little need for close supervision. Many of the employees have been with the company for a long time and the bottling plant is highly automated, so there should be little need for close supervision of those working there. According to Herzberg's motivators, if employees are able to work on their own with little supervision this can empower them, leading to improved productivity and performance.

In conclusion, I believe that the organisational structure is not helping Eastburys' performance. Workloads are not evenly spread and supervisors may not be able to communicate effectively with a team of 15 employees. However, if the managers are skilled and the employees are well motivated and carrying out similar jobs, this high span of control will not create problems and may actually improve efficiency by reducing the number of highly paid managers.

📝 The candidate shows good understanding of levels of hierarchy and spans of control and is able to apply these concepts well to the case study to illustrate the points made. The response then develops in terms of the advantages of fewer levels in the hierarchy and the positive and negative aspects of wide spans of control, demonstrating good analysis and, once again, linking this into motivational aspects. These concepts are then linked into performance issues to show judgement in the response given. The final paragraph then concludes with a well-balanced evaluation, linked effectively to Eastburys' situation.

📝 **This is a borderline A-grade answer. The candidate has sound knowledge and is able to analyse points made very well. However, there is no application to the case study in the answers to questions (b) and (c) and it therefore becomes difficult to develop evaluation fully. The candidate's mark is, however, significantly boosted by the response to question (d), which has been effectively applied to the scenario.**

Answer to Case Study 1: candidate B

(a) Interest on loan is 9% of £2 million which is £180,000. They will be making £300,000 on the investment which is a lot more so the investment is worthwhile.

📝 Unfortunately the candidate has not answered the question because they have not calculated the return on capital. However, the calculation that has been carried out does help the candidate to draw the conclusion required and so does earn limited credit.

(b) The disadvantages of on-the-job training are that it is noisy and stressful. Short cuts may be taken which can be dangerous in a factory situation where glass and heavy boxes are involved.

📝 Two disadvantages are clearly identified, but these have not been explained. The candidate has attempted to link the answer into the factory situation of Eastburys, so there is some limited application, but the response lacks analysis.

(c) Setting its own budgets could mean that the staff in the restaurant, who have more idea about the importance of each area, are better able to decide how much money to allocate to different areas. For example, it is obvious that fresh local produce is important and this may cost more, so more money should be allocated towards it. More importantly, employees will feel more in charge and this can motivate them. It may have a knock-on effect of them being less likely to leave as a result, as high labour turnover is often a sign of poor morale. If staff are more motivated, they are likely to be happier in their work and this will be evident to customers. Sales have been declining recently and this may be the reason, as no one wants to revisit a restaurant that has grumpy staff. All these factors linked to more motivation are therefore bound to have a positive effect on sales and so profits should improve.

However, there may be factors outside the control of the business. For example, there could be a rise in the price of meat which would reduce the profits unless the restaurant had more money that could be allocated towards ingredients. Also at the moment there is uncertainty in the economy and people are cutting back on luxuries, so just because the restaurant staff now set their own budgets will not necessarily mean higher profits.

e This is a sound response from this candidate, who is able to apply the case study to the question and look at both positive and negative aspects of using budgets. The candidate is able to analyse and show judgement in the response, recognising that other factors will affect profitability apart from the autonomy of budget setting.

(d) Eastburys has four sections in its organisational structure and there are different numbers of staff in each of the sections. This means that it will be easier for the personnel director to monitor the work of the two assistants than it will be for the production manager to monitor the work of all the employees in that section. The company accountant has a span of control of ten as he has the cost accountant, credit control manager and eight other staff reporting directly to him, while the production director has well over 50 people reporting directly to him. The more people you are in control of, the more difficult it is to monitor if they are working properly. However, some managers may be more skilled at doing this than others and will delegate tasks to employees. How effective this is will depend on the ability of the employees to carry out the tasks delegated to them. This could either increase performance through higher motivation with the opportunity to do more interesting work or lower performance if the tasks delegated are boring or beyond the capability of the employee.

e The candidate starts off well, identifying issues relevant to organisation structure. There is confusion regarding the meaning of span of control; however, the notion of larger numbers is then developed in the correct way to be rewarded analytical marks. There is recognition of the importance of the skills of the manager providing judgement in terms of whether this increases performance.

e **This is a C-grade answer. The candidate lacks knowledge of return on capital and is confused about spans of control, but apart from that there are no other gaps in knowledge. The response has been applied well in the answers to questions (c) and (d). The response to question (b) would be improved with further development. It is important to use the mark allocation of each question as a guide to the length of response required.**

ase study

Jacksons

Jacksons is an independent department store in its 70th year of trading. It is located in a town with a population of 100,000. Jacksons is a traditional, family-run, private limited company which has been in the family for all 70 years and five family members hold senior positions within the company. The business employs 145 staff across a range of departments, including furniture, electrical goods, lighting, kitchen equipment, china and glass, clothing, toys, accessories, cards and gifts, cosmetics and a restaurant.

The company is proud of the quality of its products and, as a member of the Association of Independent Stores, it is able to source good quality products and sell them on at reasonable prices, providing good value for money for its customers.

Jacksons is located in large premises situated in the central shopping area of the town. The store is owned by the company and has recently been valued at £4.5 million. It is the only department store in the town; the nearest competing store is 40 miles away. The building is rather cramped due to the expansion of the number of departments and the management team are starting to wonder if they are trying to offer too many different products to customers.

Over the years they have prided themselves on having excellent employer-employee relations. Apart from offering staff discounts of 15% on goods, they also have regular team meetings, delegate responsibility for setting budgets to each department and allow teams/departments to organise their own work schedules. Staff in departments are also encouraged to rotate jobs by moving to other sections every six months.

Jacksons has not experienced any human resource issues since the business began, but there have been a number of staff who have left over the last two years. This seems to have coincided with the recent establishment of an out-of-town shopping centre a few miles from the store. In 2007 18 staff left, while in 2008 staff turnover was 30 employees. Jacksons is not used to staff leaving in such high numbers and has never before paid much attention to the need to recruit staff, having generally relied on placing an advert in the shop window. However, the company is now experiencing difficulties in filling vacancies and many recently recruited employees have only stayed for a short time before leaving. There have been particular difficulties in finding suitable applicants for the role of accountant, which is starting to cause concern in the light of the company's financial worries.

The number of customer complaints has also increased over the last six months, something that Jacksons has never experienced before. The company has always prided itself on having excellent customer service. The business is now experiencing a significant decline in sales levels in some departments. If this trend continues, Jacksons will find it increasingly difficult to trade at a profit.

(a) **Calculate the percentage change in labour turnover of Jacksons from 2007 to 2008.** (5 marks)

(b) **Analyse the importance of Jacksons using non-financial methods to motivate staff.** (8 marks)

(c) **To what extent can recruitment and selection improve the effectiveness of Jacksons?** (12 marks)

(d) **Discuss how Jacksons might improve its profitability.** (15 marks)

Answer to Case Study 2: candidate A

(a) labour turnover $= \dfrac{\text{no. of employees leaving per year}}{\text{no. of employees employed that year}} \times 100$

Two years ago: $\dfrac{18}{145} \times 100 = 12.4\%$

Last year: $\dfrac{30}{145} \times 100 = 20.7\%$

Percentage change is $20.6 - 12.4 = 8.3\%$ increase in labour turnover

This is a perfect answer. The candidate has stated the formula, calculated both percentages and, importantly, recognised that the question asked for the percentage change, gained by subtracting one figure from the other.

(b) Non-financial methods are used by Jacksons as they give employees the chance to rotate jobs every six months. This means that they do not become bored with their jobs and have the chance to experience new opportunities.

Employees are also allowed to organise their own work schedules. This is a form of empowerment and would make the employees feel valued by their employer. This links in with Herzberg's theory that giving employees recognition and control over their work situation will lead to higher levels of motivation.

The candidate clearly identifies two non-financial methods used by Jacksons, showing both knowledge and application. There is some weak analysis in the first paragraph, but the second paragraph has much stronger analysis, with links to motivational theory.

(c) Recruiting the right people into the right jobs is key for any organisation. Only if it has the people with the right skills, knowledge and attributes for the job will the organisation have the chance to work as effectively as possible. Recruitment is concerned with drafting job descriptions, outlining the person required for the job (the person specification), drafting advertisements and placing them in the correct place where sufficient numbers of applicants will see the vacancy, sending out application packs (e.g. application forms to complete), carrying out shortlisting of applicants against the objective criteria in the person specification and inviting people for interview. This is where the selection process takes over, in the form of interviews and testing.

Jacksons is obviously having problems filling vacancies and keeping staff, which might mean that it hasn't recruited the right people into the jobs to start with. It would appear that the company is not experienced at this process, having relied on word of mouth in the past. It could have a better process if it used an agency to recruit on its behalf and matched the applicants more closely with the person specification and needs of the job. The company could even try headhunting. Interviewing is important and managers need to ensure that it is a thorough process so they really get to know applicants and whether they are suitable for the job. Interviews can be carried out on a one-to-one basis or by panel, as it is often better to have more than one person's viewpoint about an applicant. The more objective the process, the more likely it is that the right applicant will be recruited — and recruiting the right people into the right jobs is key for any organisation, including Jacksons.

> ✏ The candidate starts off well with an evaluative statement. Unfortunately this is not developed later on but merely repeated at the end of the response. There then follows a very detailed account of the recruitment and selection process, with no application to the case study. The candidate obviously has sound knowledge of this topic, but care should be taken to address the question from the outset or there is a danger of running out of time later in the examination. The second paragraph starts to apply this knowledge to the case study, but the candidate is focusing on how Jacksons can improve its recruitment and selection rather than focusing on how an effective process could improve the company's performance. The response then becomes much more general again and there is a lack of focus on performance issues. Unfortunately the candidate gains very few marks for this response.

(d) Jacksons could increase its profits by increasing the prices of its goods. Whether this is a realistic option would depend on many factors, including the competition and the price elasticity of demand of the products sold. The company obviously sells a huge range of products, but none of them seem to be unique to enable higher prices to be charged. There are bound to be a lot of other stores in the high street selling fashion clothes (e.g. Monsoon, Top Shop, Officers Club), as well as other retailers located at the new out-of-town shopping centre which might include electrical stores etc. If Jacksons does increase prices in such competitive markets, customers will simply stop buying from there altogether, which will in fact decrease profits even more in the long term. The elasticity of demand is probably elastic, which means that if prices were raised there would be a higher proportionate change in quantity demanded, particularly as there is so much competition. This is therefore not a realistic strategy for the company to choose.

The other option open to Jacksons would be to decrease costs and therefore achieve higher profits that way. We are told that the company is a member of

Associated Independent Stores and obtains its supplies from them. Possibly it could look into sourcing goods from cheaper suppliers, although one of its USPs appears to be good quality goods and if cheaper sources were found, quality may suffer, leading to a further drop in sales.

It is going to be quite difficult for the company to improve profits substantially in the short term and maybe a radical overhaul of the business is required to improve long-term prospects. Removing unprofitable areas of the business and expanding profitable areas might be a better option, as we are told the store is cramped. Refurbishment is probably also needed to make the outlet more modern. Although this would cost money and reduce profits in the short term, it may be what is needed to increase long-term profits. Certainly a radical approach is called for if Jacksons wants to survive, let alone be profitable in such competitive markets.

🖉 A very good start to this question, clearly explaining increasing prices as an option, applying it well to the case study and analysing with good use of theory (e.g. price elasticity of demand). The candidate then goes on to evaluate the likelihood of this strategy being a success and improving profitability. The second paragraph explains decreasing costs as an alternative option, which again is well applied, developed and evaluated in terms of the question asked. Finally the candidate recognises that the business may need a radical overhaul to increase profits in the long term and recognises the importance of differentiating between short-term and long-term profitability.

🖉 **This is an A-grade answer overall. The candidate has produced good answers to questions (a), (b) and (d), which compensate for the response to question (c). The latter illustrates how candidates can sometimes lose focus on a question when they know a lot about a topic. The response to question (d) is particularly strong in terms of knowledge, application, analysis and evaluation, and demonstrates how focusing on the exact wording of the question from the outset can help to achieve a good grade.**

Answer to Case Study 2: candidate B

(a) Last year it was 12%, this year it is 21%.

🖉 The candidate has rounded the percentages, which is acceptable although answers to one decimal place are often preferred. Luckily both answers are correct, as no workings have been shown. Because they are correct, it is assumed that the candidate does know the formula and what to do with the figures. If, however, the candidate had made an arithmetical error and got the wrong answers, no credit would be given as the examiner would not be able to follow the logic, in the absence of any calculations. It is always advisable for candidates to state the formula and show workings in case a wrong button on the calculator is pressed, as some marks could then be awarded rather than none. The candidate has also

case
study

not given the percentage change in the response, so would not gain the relevant mark for this.

(b) Non-financial methods used by Jacksons would include empowerment — letting employees set their own work schedules, teamworking and consultation, which Jacksons does by getting employees in their teams to have meetings — and job rotation, which it does by moving employees between departments. Financial methods used are the 15% staff discounts on goods sold in the store.

> The candidate starts off well by identifying non-financial methods used and linking these into the case study. However, these points are not developed in terms of how they motivate or the importance of them as motivational factors, and the response therefore lacks analysis. The candidate then goes on to look at financial motivators, which is not required in the question.

(c) At the moment it would appear that Jacksons has little knowledge of how to recruit staff as few staff have left the organisation in the past. Certainly relying on notices in a window is not a very professional approach, and it would not be the best way to get the right people into the right jobs. This might be one of the reasons why people are leaving, because they are not suited to the job and don't have the correct skills for it.

Effective recruitment and selection is about having an objective process where the organisation has thought about the job clearly (job description) and the person needed to fill it (person specification). Maybe the reason the company cannot recruit someone into accounts is because it is not advertising in the right place.

If the right people are in the right jobs then issues like poor customer service would not arise because employees would have the right skills and attributes for the job.

Obviously Jacksons is having trouble recruiting an accountant. If the company used an agency or even a headhunter, it could have more success — and this is an important role to fill as there are problems with finances at the moment. If a person was recruited into this role, this could help to turn the business's finances around and improve performance. However, as things are going badly, it is questionable whether effective recruitment on its own will be enough — but at least it is a start and will prevent further deterioration of the company's position.

> The candidate's response is linked into the organisation from the start and is developed in terms of effectiveness of the current process. It is applied to Jacksons throughout and judgement is made as to whether the various measures will lead to improved performance of the company, making this a good response.

(d) Jacksons could improve its profits by selling off its fixed assets (e.g. the building is worth £4.5 million). Maybe it could use sale and leaseback because this would provide the company with more cash and still allow it to keep using the store. Alternatively, it could get a bank loan and increase profits that way, although it may in fact decrease profits as interest would have to be paid on the loan. If

Jacksons could arrange credit facilities for its stock buying, this would also increase profits in the short term as the company wouldn't have to pay for them for a while.

On the other hand, Jacksons could improve profitability by increasing its prices or decreasing its costs. This would be difficult to do as there is so much competition in the high street and out-of-town stores and it is probably tied into a contract with AIS so couldn't get supplies elsewhere.

The candidate has unfortunately confused profit with cash flow and given a detailed account of how to improve cash flow rather than on how to improve profitability. This first paragraph is therefore not worth any marks. The second paragraph does contain valid points, which are briefly applied with some limited judgement. The candidate would therefore pick up some marks for this section. There is no negative marking and so irrelevant sections are just ignored.

The candidate has achieved a borderline C/D grade overall. There is a good response to question (c) and question (a) earns good marks, in spite of the poor exam technique. The response to question (b) lacked development and was far too brief. Question (d) went off at a tangent at the start. Candidates need to be careful to know the difference between key terms such as profitability and cash flow.

BMW Mini

Since its launch in 2001, the new BMW-owned Mini has gone from strength to strength. The reasons for this are numerous but include a fully automated, state-of-the-art production process, excellent quality assurance systems, good links with suppliers, flexible work practices and high levels of capacity utilisation. In April 2007 the one millionth Mini came off the production line at Oxford.

The company operates a three-shift system to enable the plant to have the capacity to work 24/7. The high levels of capacity utilisation are evident as in 1999, 3,500 workers produced 56,000 Rover cars at the plant, whereas in 2007, 4,500 Mini workers were producing 200,000 Minis.

In 2000 BMW invested £230 million in the Oxford plant to ensure that it installed the most advanced manufacturing facilities. This was followed by a further investment of £100 million in 2005. Further investment was needed to increase output levels due to the huge level of demand for the new cars and to try to reduce customer waiting times.

The company aims to be as responsive to customer demand as possible and ensure that vehicles are built to the customers' specification. Customers are able to choose from a range of different exteriors, roofs, upholstery and other equipment. Cars are available in a range of colours and the Mini Cooper models have contrasting roof colours in black or white. Customers can even design their own Mini online using computer packages.

The body shop in the factory is highly automated, using hundreds of robots to assemble body panels and weld together body parts of the Mini. This process is integrated and coordinated by a sophisticated information technology system which ensures that processes are carried out in the correct order and that quality is maintained throughout the process. Any problems are identified immediately and rectified rather than being carried on to the next assembly stage. This is part of the zero-fault quality programme which ensures high quality standards throughout the production process.

(a) Assuming that the maximum capacity utilisation of the plant is 224,000, calculate the capacity utilisation of the Mini plant in 2007. (2 marks)

(b) Explain the impact of an increase in capacity utilisation for BMW at the Mini plant. (5 marks)

(c) Analyse two advantages of BMW having high levels of customer service. (7 marks)

(d) To what extent does the quality system used by BMW at the Mini plant affect sales of Mini cars? (13 marks)

(e) Discuss the extent to which the use of robotics at the Mini plant might improve the operational efficiency of the business. (13 marks)

Answer to Case Study 3: candidate A

(a) capacity utilisation $= \dfrac{200,000}{224,000} \times 100 = 89.3\%$

> 🗭 The candidate has correctly calculated the capacity utilisation. It is useful to show workings rather than just state percentages in case an error is made in the calculation. Some credit will be gained for use of correct figures.

(b) Capacity utilisation is the percentage of the firm's maximum productivity level that is being achieved. Increases in capacity utilisation lead to a reduction in fixed costs per unit and an increase in profit levels for the company. When Rover cars were being manufactured at the plant, the capacity utilisation was only 25%. Under BMW it's now 64% more, which means that BMW has the potential to make higher profits at the plant.

Although higher levels of capacity utilisation can mean that workers are more stressed as they have to work at a faster rate, this probably is not the case at the Mini plant. The increase in capacity utilisation is probably down to more investment in new technology.

> 🗭 An excellent response, showing the importance of knowing key definitions. This has been well applied by the candidate, who has also calculated the previous capacity utilisation correctly. In addition, the candidate has explained how an increase impacts positively and negatively on a business. Positive and negative aspects are not needed to gain full marks — these would have been awarded on the basis of the first paragraph.

(c) High levels of customer service can mean that BMW gains a good reputation and a good image, which in turn means that customers will return and buy another car in the future. However, this does lead to higher costs for the business, which could reduce the levels of profit made overall. Because the Mini has such a good reputation, people have to wait for their cars as they are made to order.

> 🗭 The candidate starts off well and identifies several advantages of good reputation, good image and customer loyalty. However, the response then goes on to cover disadvantages, which are not required. The response also lacks application to the case study, as the mere mention of BMW and Mini do not attract application marks. Application needs to be developed in the context of the case study. The candidate does apply the case study at the end of the response, but this is not linked into advantages and gains no credit.

(d) BMW operates a quality system which focuses on ensuring that faults are identified early on in the process and rectified at that point, avoiding the need for high levels of waste and scrap that lead to increased costs. It appears that the system used is a combination of both quality assurance and quality control as there are quality checks carried out at the end of each process, which is the best of both worlds. If

BMW can ensure zero-fault quality, this will ensure that there are fewer problems with vehicles. This will add further to its high levels of focus on customer satisfaction and people will buy more Minis as a result.

In the past, the British car industry had a reputation for poor quality and this impacted heavily on sales. A focus on quality is now recognised as a vital factor in staying ahead of the competition in most industries, and the car industry is no exception with so much competition from companies renowned for their quality such as Honda. BMW therefore had no choice but to adapt and survive.

There is therefore no doubt that the quality system does have a huge impact on the sales of Minis. However, BMW has also recognised that the whole package of carrying out market research, developing trendy designs for its products and having a highly committed workforce, together with the quality of the finished car, all lead to the creation of a USP. All of these factors together are important for the long-term success of the business.

> ℓ A superb response. The candidate shows clear understanding of the key terms at the start of the response. This is well applied to BMW and the car industry throughout. The answer is developed to show clear analysis in terms of the effect increased quality can have on sales. It is clearly evaluative throughout and concludes with further evaluation in the form of recognising that other factors could also contribute to overall sales and success of the company.

(e) The use of a highly automated production facility is bound to ensure that quality levels are higher. As BMW has hundreds of robots at its Mini plant, there is less reliance on manual labour. However, although labour costs are reduced, this is counteracted by the huge cost of this equipment (£230 million plus a further £100 million in 2005), so both long-term and short-term costs will be high. Nevertheless, the positive effects of increased productivity and reduction in waste are bound to lead to reduced costs. More importantly, the quality issues that BMW stresses are vitally important are more likely to be achieved through the use of robotics. These factors all have a positive effect on overall sales and profitability.

Although initially there may have been concerns over job losses, this has clearly not happened as the plant is now employing 1,000 workers more than it was under Rover, despite being more technically innovative. Therefore any potential decrease in productivity because of a possible decrease in motivation has clearly not occurred and productivity levels have increased, further increasing the overall efficiency. No doubt the use of robotics helped the company also to achieve zero defects and to increase capacity utilisation to 89%; this also demonstrates high levels of efficiency.

> ℓ Another excellent response. This shows good application to the case study, drawing out relevant data on employee numbers and cost of technology, as well as linking into zero faults. The effects of robotics have been analysed through identifying positive factors and potential drawbacks in terms of financial and

human resource costs. The candidate has also linked back to earlier responses on quality and capacity utilisation. The importance of relevant factors is weighed up to demonstrate sound judgement and an overall conclusion is reached.

📝 **This is an outstanding A-grade answer, in which the candidate shows good knowledge and uses the text extremely well to illustrate relevant points. The candidate demonstrates a good use of theory and writes the responses analytically, providing evidence of judgement throughout. Apart from covering negative aspects in question (c) and failing to apply this response sufficiently, the candidate has shown excellent interpretation of the questions throughout.**

Answer to Case Study 3: candidate B

(a) Capacity utilisation = $\dfrac{4,500}{200,000}$ = 44 cars produced by each worker

📝 The candidate gains no marks here because of incorrect working. It is important to learn formulae, as ability to carry out calculations will be required.

(b) Capacity utilisation is to do with the number of workers employed and how they are used. From the figures we can see that workers were producing 16 cars for Rover and are producing 44 cars for Mini. This means that fixed costs per car will be reduced now as more cars are being produced.

📝 This response shows the difficulty candidates experience when they don't know the key terminology. The candidate struggles to produce a valid response for this question but does hit on reduction of fixed costs per car at the end of the response, so would be given some credit on a 'benefit of the doubt' basis.

(c) High levels of customer service mean that customers are happy with the service provided. This has probably led to the huge increase in the sales of the Mini as 'the company aims to be as responsive to customer demand as possible and ensure that vehicles are built to the customers' specification'. It has created a USP and this is probably why sales have continued to rise every year and also why it should ensure the business has a long-term future.

📝 The candidate starts with a basic idea of customer service, though in the main this is repeating the words in the question. There is recognition that there is a direct link between improved customer service and an increase in sales, providing some basic analysis and some limited application. The next section would appear to be further application, but it is lifted straight from the text without explaining its significance for the question. Consequently, no application marks will be awarded here.

(d) BMW uses a zero-fault quality programme which means that it wants to ensure no faults. Quality is important if you want to sell your products as no one wants to buy products that are faulty. Once a company gets a reputation for selling faulty goods, the word gets around and people will not buy those products and sales will fall. Therefore by BMW ensuring zero faults people will be happier and sales will rise. There are a lot of car manufacturers out there and so if BMW is going to compete with Ford, Toyota etc. it has to make sure the quality of its cars is good as otherwise customers will choose these companies' products over BMW's.

> The response starts quite vaguely but does develop the issue of reputation and the impact this has on sales, attempting to apply this to the car industry in terms of the competition. There is therefore some application, analysis and evaluation present but this needs further development and there is no recognition of the overall significance of quality in terms of its effect on sales.

(e) The use of robots in the manufacture of cars can improve quality, increase the amount of cars that can be produced and decrease the costs of production, leading to higher profit levels. Robots are generally more effective than people and as BMW uses hundreds of them, the company is likely to be much more efficient overall.

However, the equipment does cost a lot of money, over £230 million in 2000. It also costs a lot to maintain this equipment and this expenditure will reduce the levels of profit for the business.

Workers at BMW may also fear for their jobs and this could lead to a decrease in motivation. According to Maslow's hierarchy of needs, if employees are feeling insecure they will not be motivated and can become less productive. Consequently the business will not be as efficient as it used to be.

> The candidate mentions a lot of valid positive points in the first paragraph but does not develop these points. The second paragraph focuses on profitability rather than efficiency, although there is recognition of the cost of robotic equipment. The third paragraph shows valid development of negative factors, with the candidate linking human resource issues into operations management.

> **This is a solid D-grade answer. The candidate shows some lack of knowledge of key terms, such as capacity utilisation, and therefore is unable to gain marks. Luckily in this case study, these were lower mark questions, so the candidate was not unduly penalised. However, if they had been the higher mark questions, the candidate would have struggled to gain marks, showing the importance of knowledge of terminology. Although the responses to the last three questions start vaguely, they do develop into valid responses so the candidate is able to pick up marks here.**

Cadbury

Cadbury has been in existence for over 100 years and has been producing Cadbury Dairy Milk since 1905. It has approximately 32% of the confectionery market's total annual sales of about £5.9 billion. Customers spend about £1 million a day on Cadbury Dairy Milk in the UK.

In 2003 mother branding was introduced, with Cadbury using Cadbury Dairy Milk and Flake as mother brands. The Flake mother brand encompassed the traditional Flake, along with Flake Dark, Flake Dipped, Flake Praline and Snow Flake. Wispa was replaced by Cadbury Dairy Milk Bubbly and Cadbury Caramel by Cadbury Dairy Milk with Caramel. A large number of other products were also launched under this Cadbury Dairy Milk mother brand. Cadbury aimed to create product equilibrium by redesigning wrappers. By standardising packaging for all its Cadbury Dairy Milk products, it created a 'purple patch' on the shelves. It was hoped that the greater visual impact created would encourage customers to buy Cadbury over other brands, especially as 60%–70% of chocolate is bought on impulse. Cadbury is careful to keep a close eye on competitors and their products, and it uses competitor-based pricing where it aims to match its prices with those of competitors in the market (e.g. Cadbury Dairy Milk matched with Galaxy and Flake with Ripple, both manufactured by Mars).

Cadbury does not use the Boston matrix in its marketing strategy, and uses brand positioning instead. It has 'drive brands' such as Cadbury Dairy Milk, Flake, Turkish Delight, Snaps and Cadbury Creme Egg, which equate with cash cows in the Boston matrix. 'Build brands', such as Trident, Bourneville Dark and Green & Black's, could equate with rising stars or question marks. Products seen as dogs are eliminated (e.g. Fuse in 1996).

In 2005 Cadbury bought Green & Black's, a successful business well known for making high quality, intense flavour chocolate using only organic ingredients. This is marketed as a stand-alone brand, aimed at the luxury end of the confectionery market. There is no purple packaging or Cadbury label present on these chocolate bars.

The years 2007/2008 saw the launch of two distinctive and different advertising campaigns by Cadbury. After ditching the Cadbury Flake Girl in 2004, she was revitalised in the form of supermodel Alyssa Sutherland in 2007 in a £5 million advertising campaign. This campaign was, however, short lived and in March 2008 singer Joss Stone became the new face of Cadbury Flake. The advert departs from previous Flake advertisements and is in a documentary style. Joss Stone takes a break from recording in a studio, picks up a Flake and sings the well-known Flake jingle, which was first created in 1920.

The year 2007 also saw the end of Cadbury's 11-year, £10 million sponsorship of *Coronation Street* and the launch of a radical advertising campaign. The commercial does not show chocolate or even mention the word but instead shows a drumming gorilla playing 'In the Air Tonight', a Phil Collins song. This £9 million advertising campaign sees Cadbury moving away from traditional methods of advertising that focus on the product and its taste and concentrate instead on creating an impact.

(a) Explain briefly how Cadbury might use its marketing in order to keep its high market share in the chocolate market. (6 marks)

(b) Analyse two reasons why Cadbury sells Green & Black's under a different brand name. (7 marks)

(c) Is the price elasticity of demand for Cadbury's chocolate products price elastic or price inelastic? Justify your view. (12 marks)

(d) Discuss the extent to which Cadbury's current promotional campaigns might improve sales of its products. (15 marks)

Answer to Case Study 4: candidate A

(a) Cadbury has stayed dominant in the chocolate market because it has paid close attention to all the elements of its marketing mix. It has continually looked for new ways to develop its products to ensure people buy them, such as the use of mother branding (e.g. Cadbury Dairy Milk) and altering the look of its products so that the purple packaging stands out from the competition. The company has also recognised the importance of promotion through advertising and sponsorship of *Coronation Street*, so that the products stay in the public's eye. It ensures its products are competitively priced (e.g. Flake priced the same as Ripple) and sells the products in many different places (e.g. supermarkets, garages, internet) so it is easy for people to buy them.

 An excellent response using the elements of the marketing mix to demonstrate how Cadbury has kept its dominant position in the market. The answer is well applied to Cadbury and its products.

(b) Cadbury sells Green & Black's under a different brand name because it wants to create a unique selling point (USP) and aim at a niche market. The USP comes from the organic ingredients used. This adds value and allows for product differentiation and premium pricing to be used, as many customers are seeking to buy organic products and there are few organic chocolates to choose from. This then allows higher profits to be made, because Green & Black's is aimed at the luxury end of the market at people with higher incomes and/or a particular lifestyle, e.g. only buy organic products. These people are prepared to pay more because they can afford to or because they believe organic products are worth paying more for. Cadbury can therefore charge higher prices for these products than if they carried the Cadbury logo, which is associated with mass-produced chocolate. These higher prices would not be possible if the company instead launched organic chocolate under the Cadbury Dairy Milk mother brand.

 An excellent analysis of two reasons, with very good linking into the mother brand and mass market concepts.

(c) Price elasticity of demand measures the responsiveness of demand to a change in price. If a small percentage change in price leads to a larger percentage change in the quantity demanded, then demand is price elastic. Inelastic demand is when the change in quantity is a lower percentage than the change in price.

To a certain extent Cadbury uses price skimming with its Green & Black's range and is able to do this due to the added value created by the organic and luxury USPs. This suggests that demand is price inelastic, as Green & Black's customers will pay a high price because of the USP. With Cadbury's other brands there is no evidence of price skimming on its main products, although boxes of chocolates, given as gifts, probably have inelastic demand too. High prices for brands such as Roses do not seem to lead to a significant fall in demand.

Although sales of Cadbury products are high, if the company did adopt a strategy of price skimming for Cadbury Dairy Milk, it might find that people would switch to buying products from Mars or Nestlé instead. The confectionery market doesn't really lend itself to this strategy due to the high degree of competition in the market — the chocolate market is an oligopoly with similar, but differentiated products. Although there is some loyalty to Cadbury, if Cadbury adopted price skimming it could see customers switch to other brands, sales fall and profitability decline as a result, especially as 60–70% of chocolate is bought on impulse. I think that demand for chocolate is very price elastic and any increase in price would lead to a greater percentage change in the quantity demanded. This is because there are a number of alternative products supplied by other chocolate manufacturers. Therefore this strategy would not be a viable one for Cadbury to pursue.

In general most Cadbury chocolates have price elastic demand because they are not a necessity and there are close substitutes. However, some customers may feel that there is no alternative to Green & Black's organic chocolate, especially as chocolate is habit forming. For these reasons, a minority of Cadbury's products will have inelastic demand.

> 🖉 The response starts well by accurately defining the concept. It then starts to talk about pricing strategy, but immediately links this to price inelastic demand in an evaluative way. This second paragraph develops the skimming strategy with good analysis of price elasticity of demand and is well applied to Cadbury. This analysis is then contrasted with further examples that suggest price elastic demand for other products. The final paragraph concludes by linking individual Cadbury brands to the factors that influence elasticity, leading to a pertinent conclusion.

(d) The promotional campaigns Cadbury is using are above-the-line promotion. Advertising can be informative or persuasive and aim to raise awareness of the product to increase brand loyalty.

Cadbury has launched two new campaigns. It appears to have spent a lot of money on advertising, but many people objected to the Flake girl adverts as they were seen as sexist and suggestive. This may have had a negative effect on sales as a result. However, the aim of the company's advertising is to remind us about established products, and the Cadbury Flake jingle has obviously lasted longer than Alyssa Sutherland, the last Flake girl. With so much competition in the market place, customers do need to be reminded constantly about products, otherwise the chances are that they will switch brands.

The gorilla advert has certainly made an impact and has been greatly talked about. Although there is no mention of chocolate and no chocolate bar in the advert, it clearly shows the glass-and-a-half production logo and the purple colour of the CDM brand. This persuasively reminds us about Cadbury and keeps the brand in the public eye, while at the same time providing some fun entertainment. Some people couldn't see the relevance of the advert, but I doubt it would put them off eating Cadbury chocolate.

Many would say it was a risky strategy for Cadbury to pull out of its *Coronation Street* sponsorship, which ensured regular television coverage of the brand at peak viewing times several times a week. Regular reminders often work well to keep the brand in the public eye. What Cadbury needs to ensure is that it doesn't replace customers with new ones, but keeps old customers and attracts new ones, to make sure sales continue to rise. Cadbury certainly cannot afford not to advertise if it wants to remain in the public eye and be certain of its continued 32% of the confectionery market.

> 🖉 The candidate starts off well with a definition of advertising and an explanation of the purpose. The candidate explains each promotional strategy with excellent application and explores the positive and negative implications, coming to the conclusion that the basis of the advertising is to keep the brand in the public eye.

> 🖉 **This is a top A-grade answer, earning maximum marks. The candidate has made excellent use of the text, illustrating how effective use of the text can enhance a response. The candidate has also shown a good use of theory and often starts a response with a definition of key terms. Responses are written analytically, with evidence of judgement being shown throughout. No time has been lost on irrelevant responses; the candidate was able to deliver high quality answers to every question.**

Answer to Case Study 4: candidate B

(a) Cadbury has stayed dominant due to the excellent brand image it has built up over 100 years and because the quality of its products is good. The company spends a lot of money on advertising, the recent campaign costing £9 million. These factors mean that people will continue to buy because of the good quality and they are constantly reminded about Cadbury because of the advertising so they don't switch to another product.

> 🖉 This is a solid but brief response, clearly explaining potential reasons for Cadbury's continued dominance. It is also well applied to Cadbury.

(b) Cadbury sells this chocolate under another brand name because it is a luxury product and the company can charge more money for it if it is marketed in this way. Cadbury can also stress that it is an organic range of chocolate, which might be lost if the company tried to market it under the Cadbury brand.

> Two reasons have been identified and explained with some application to Cadbury. However, the response needs to be developed much more for reasonable analysis marks to be awarded.

(c) Cadbury matches its product prices with the prices of similar products in the marketplace, because higher prices will lead to a big fall in demand. For Green & Black's, the price elasticity of demand means that it can charge a higher price.

> This is a very ambiguous answer. At no stage is there any indication of the meaning of price elasticity of demand. The answer is based on extracts from the case study and general knowledge, but there is no attempt at analysis. The candidate would gain a very limited reward for this answer.

(d) Many people thought the gorilla advert was stupid because it says nothing about chocolate. However, everyone was talking about it, which is one of the aims of advertising — to get the company noticed so that people will buy its products.

The Joss Stone advert is also a different style to the previous Flake Girl adverts, in the hope that it may appeal to a younger audience who might start to buy Flake as a result of associating it with Joss Stone. The same reason could be applied to stopping promotion of *Coronation Street*, which is watched by older people.

If both these things happen, sales should increase. Cadbury obviously thinks it is worthwhile as it has spent millions of pounds on these campaigns. A company as established as Cadbury wouldn't do it if it thought it was a waste of money.

> This response has been well applied to Cadbury and in the first paragraph the aim of advertising is covered. The candidate has mentioned all the recent campaigns and there is some limited development of the points by looking at the positive and negative implications. Attempts have been made to link this into sales, showing limited judgement in the conclusions reached. However, the response is brief overall and needed further development to gain higher analysis and evaluation marks.

> **This is an E-grade response. The candidate has shown weakness in a number of areas of knowledge and limited analysis in the first three answers. There has been more success in application to the case study, and the answer to question (d) shows sound analysis and some evaluation with the application. This is sufficient to raise the overall standard of the paper to a pass level.**

Pret A Manger

Pret A Manger (Pret) began in 1986 when two friends borrowed £17,000 to open up a sandwich shop in London. Their idea was to sell freshly made, organic sandwiches. Today there are over 160 branches in the UK, mainly in London.

Pret created a niche market, adding quality and unusual fillings to a previously predictable and stagnant market. In 2007 Pret's annual sales were £220 million and it recorded a net profit of £23 million. According to Jim Winship, Director of the British Sandwich Association, Pret set the standard but other brands have, to some degree, caught up. 'It is a highly competitive market, particularly with the coffee bar sector having a great deal more activity recently.' It is a tough market and not so easy to innovate any more.

In the UK Pret is growing strongly, with 45 new outlets opened in the last two years. It has also recently launched a new concept — the 'Pret Pod'. This is a kiosk-style satellite branch, in busy locations such as stations and airports. The 'Pods' will use kitchens at nearby branches to prepare their stock.

Pret works on a relatively low marketing budget — it amounts to just 0.4% of total sales. There are only three people in the marketing department, not much for a company whose financial target is a net profit margin of 9%.

Promotions largely consist of posters in shop windows, chatty copyrighting on the packaging and a brochure. Commercial director, Simon Hargraves, says that 'We don't do advertising and we have no press office — we sell sandwiches. We try to keep it as simple as that. All of our sandwiches are made on the day of purchase and at the location of sale: consequently there are no "sell by" dates.'

Pret selects its workforce carefully, picking only one in every 14 job applicants. Potential recruits are sent on a one-day experience in a branch, where staff members vote on whether to employ the applicant or not. Employees are encouraged to take responsibility for their own role within a branch and there is a strong emphasis on teamwork, both within shops and between neighbouring shops. Some training, emphasising the aims and values of Pret, is run at the company's specialist Training Academy in Victoria, but most is on the job. Internal recruitment is used a great deal for positions of responsibility.

Customer service is very important. Mystery shoppers are used to check service, such as the target to serve coffee within 60 seconds of the order. In addition stores are regularly checked for safety, hygiene and quality.

Staff are encouraged to suggest ideas to improve the company and financial rewards are given for good ideas. Twice a year a 'massive party' is organised for the workforce. Pay is set at a level of £1 per hour higher than the industry average and hours are flexible, to suit staff needs. Pret was rated as the best catering employer by the *Sunday*

Times. Pret's labour turnover is high at 90%, but much lower than the industry average of 265%. For managers it is only 14%.

(a) Based on the figures in the case study, did Pret achieve its financial target of a 9% net profit margin? (5 marks)

(b) Analyse two reasons why Pret has such a low marketing budget. (8 marks)

(c) To what extent do the methods employed by Pret enable it to meet customer expectations? (12 marks)

(d) Evaluate the evidence that Pret is using theories of motivation in order to develop and retain its workforce. (15 marks)

Answer to Case Study 5: candidate A

(a) net profit margin $= \dfrac{\text{net profit}}{\text{annual sales}} \times 100 = \dfrac{£23m}{£220m} \times 100 = 10.5\%$

The target net profit margin was 9% and so Pret has exceeded its target.

Candidate A has shown good technique in starting with the formula for net profit margin. This guarantees some credit, even if the subsequent answer does not apply the numbers correctly. Candidate A then goes on to use the right figures and calculates the correct answer of 10.5%. In a question such as this, there is a tendency for candidates to leave the answer at 10.5%. Given the wording of the question, the final sentence is required in order to secure the final mark, as this is needed to show that the target of 9% has been met or surpassed.

(b) One reason why Pret works on a low marketing budget is because of the high quality of its products. There are no 'sell by' dates and so fresh produce made on the day of consumption is one of Pret's guarantees. The sandwich market is not one in which there are many organic sandwich makers and so Pret has a unique selling point for its products. This attracts customers who are looking for organic products. As the customers are actively seeking Pret's products, there is less need for heavy promotion and advertising. By carefully selecting its employees and thus ensuring the quality of its products, Pret does not need to spend money on promotions.

The second reason for Pret's low marketing budget is the high level of competition within the market, particularly the coffee bar sector. Because it is a tough market, there is no point in Pret spending a lot of money on promotion, as it is hard to gain extra sales from more well-established brands such as Starbucks.

The third reason for Pret's low marketing budget is the high level of word-of-mouth advertising that it receives. Most of its branches are in London and so customers are likely to see different branches. The close proximity of its branches will mean that there will be high levels of brand awareness in the London area. For this reason the main promotions are just posters in shop windows. These will be seen frequently by potential customers and therefore there is no need to use more expensive forms of advertising media.

There are two very good explanations given in this response. The first paragraph contains an excellent analysis of the nature of a unique selling point within a niche market. In effect, Candidate A is saying that the product is sufficiently attractive to require relatively little marketing. The third reason also shows good logical thinking and is almost certainly derived from the candidate having some understanding of Pret's existence in London. Although most application will come from the case study or article in the examination paper, this third paragraph shows how a person can draw upon their own understanding of the world of business in order to apply their answer. The argument presented in the second paragraph, however, is not a valid reason for a lower marketing budget and therefore would receive no credit whatsoever. Many students assume that the examiner is instructed to read the first two reasons only (as the question only asks for two reasons) and ignore the third reason. This is not the case. Examiners are instructed to read all of the answer and credit the best parts. Therefore the second paragraph would be ignored and suitable credit given to paragraphs 1 and 3, as they are the only parts of the answer that are relevant. Marks are not deducted for errors and so this answer would achieve maximum marks, despite the totally spurious argument in paragraph 2. The view of the examination board is that Candidate A has been penalised by wasting time on this paragraph and may therefore not be able to deliver such high quality answers later in the paper, when time is running short.

(c) Customer expectations are what people think should happen and how they think they should be treated when asking for or receiving customer service.

Customer expectations are based on:
- what people hear and see
- what customers read and what organisations tell them about their service
- what happens during the customer experience
- what has happened to them in previous customer service experiences

The greater the expectations that are built up by these factors, the higher the level of service that must be provided in order to meet the customers' desires.

The main customer priorities/expectations are as follows:
- High quality products or services. Pret delivers high quality products by ensuring that they are freshly made. The sandwiches are organic and made on the day of consumption. Because they are produced in the kitchen within the same outlet, there is a further reassurance that they are fresh.
- Having friendly staff dealing with the processing of the good or service. Pret staff are chosen by their fellow employees and so it is likely that the staff will get on together in a happy environment. This should make the shoppers' experiences favourable as well. Probably the most important method used by Pret to ensure that it meets customer expectations is the use of mystery shoppers to check the quality of service and the promptness of delivery of the product.

Pret was rated as the best catering employer by the *Sunday Times* and although this does not directly affect customers, a happy workforce is likely to be providing a better service, although a 90% labour turnover may indicate that there are some staffing problems that might affect customer service.

Finally, there is a specialist training academy in Victoria which helps to make sure that employees are fully trained in their jobs. This is then backed up by on-the-job training.

Overall I believe that it does meet the customers' expectations. The company is growing rapidly, despite a limited marketing budget, and has a reputation for high quality products. The fact that Pret can sell its sandwiches at such high prices suggests that customers believe they are of good quality. By picking only one in every 14 job applicants, Pret is guaranteeing high quality service, as it is being very selective in its employees. This along with its training and constant checks by the mystery shoppers are the main reasons why I believe that Pret is meeting its customers' expectations.

> An excellent answer. The student starts by defining 'customer expectations'. Not only does this earn content marks, but also it helps the examiner to see how the subsequent arguments are linked in to Pret's attempts to meet its customers' expectations. After the initial definition the answer becomes rather analytical, with no direct reference to Pret in the early part of the answer. Once the candidate moves on to discussing the quality and freshness of the sandwiches, application marks can be awarded. In the third paragraph there is some evaluation shown, where the candidate indicates why he/she believes the mystery shopper to be a key element of meeting customer expectations. However, this is the only instance of evaluation up until the final paragraph. In this final paragraph there is an excellent overall judgement made and Candidate A moves on to full marks for evaluation, having already achieved full marks for the other skills of knowledge, application and analysis.

(d) Pret is using both Theory X and Theory Y styles of management.

Pret pays its workers higher wages than the industry average and makes sure that the sandwiches are made in the correct, most efficient way. These two factors suggest that a Theory X style of leadership or management is being used.

However, the company also gives responsibility to its workers. This would happen under a Theory Y manager. The strong emphasis on teamwork noted both within shops and between neighbouring shops is also a feature of Theory Y.

Overall there is no one theory of motivation that seems to dominate Pret's approach as it uses both Theory X and Theory Y leadership styles.

> Unfortunately this answer receives no marks. Candidate A has made a common error — confusing leadership/management styles with theories of motivation. Although there is overlap between these two topics, they are not the same thing.

Theories of motivation look at factors that encourage workers to apply themselves effectively within the workplace; leadership/ management styles study the ways in which managers organise and lead their subordinates. As the answer only ever refers to management/leadership styles and there is no reference to any theory of motivation, no credit can be given. This is probably the answer of an A2 student, as leadership is not included in the AS specification.

Candidate A achieves a B grade because three of the four questions are dealt with excellently. Some time would have been lost by the approach used in (b), but it turned out to be a wise move as the second argument was considered to be invalid and so the additional idea earned credit. There is no evidence towards the end of the paper that the candidate was running short of time at the end of the examination. The new specification offers longer time in the AS examination papers and so therefore time pressure should be less of an issue.

Answer to Case Study 5: candidate B

(a) net profit margin $= \dfrac{\text{net profit}}{\text{annual sales}} \times 100 = \dfrac{220}{23} = 9.56$

Candidate B has stated the correct formula but then makes an error by inverting the figures. Credit will be given for the formula but not for the calculation, which is incorrect. This shows that it is important to state the formula in case errors are made later in the answer. No stated formula would have meant no marks here.

(b) Pret has a low marketing budget because it has been well established since 1986 and now feels that because it is so well known it no longer needs to spend as much money on marketing. Secondly it has a low budget because it feels that customers are loyal.

The candidate makes a valid point regarding reputation with some linking into the case study and some basic analysis. The second point is also valid but is not developed and not applied to evidence from the case study, so gains only knowledge marks.

(c) Customer expectations means ensuring the needs of every single customer are met by selling what they want, making sure products are of high quality and that staff are friendly and helpful. Pret achieves this by monitoring the service by using mystery shoppers and checking the stores regularly for safety etc. Mystery shoppers pretend to be real customers buying a sandwich and drink and they feed back on how effectively they were dealt with. If they have any problems, I expect these are fed back to the shop to do something about it. Also if staff know mystery shoppers are used, it keeps them on their toes as any customer they serve could be one. This then ensures customer expectations are met.

The response starts with a definition of customer expectations and links this into how Pret monitors this through mystery shoppers, clearly applying it to the scenario. The answer though is quite brief and descriptive with limited analysis and evaluation and unfortunately only one method has been explained, when the question asked for methods. Higher marks could therefore have been achieved by explaining other methods and further development of the response.

(d) Pret gives employees responsibility for their roles in a branch and uses internal recruitment for positions of responsibility. These measures tie in with Herzberg's motivational factors, as they will motivate employees if they are being empowered and given opportunities for advancement. They also satisfy Maslow's higher level needs which some people want to achieve, such as esteem needs and maybe even self-actualisation.

The strong emphasis on teamwork at Pret ties in with Mayo's theory regarding the importance of teams and recognition given by managers to employees, the Hawthorne effect. This will motivate employees because they feel management is taking an interest in them.

Pay is £1 an hour higher than the industry average, which applies to Taylor's theory of economic man — that money is an important motivator for staff (although Herzberg would say it doesn't motivate but just prevents dissatisfaction).

As labour turnover is lower at Pret (90%) than the industry average (265%), this may be a direct effect of the attention to key motivational issues in terms of opportunities for advancement and responsibility, and Pret seem to be using a range of techniques put forward by a number of theorists in motivating its staff.

📝 This is an excellent response. Each paragraph takes a technique being used by Pret and links it into a motivational theorist showing sound knowledge, application and analysis. There are elements of judgement throughout and a link into retention in the conclusion.

📝 **This is a C grade, saved by the candidate's very good response to question (d). The mark would have been higher if the candidate had developed responses to questions (b) and (c) more fully. The mistake in the calculation in question (a) shows the need to take care when putting figures into an equation.**

Crisis? What crisis?

Last year

Narinder discovered the bad news on returning from India. She had spent a week making new contacts and finding new suppliers for her textile factory in Slough.

She had not revealed that she was considering opening up a factory in India. As the main shareholder, she did not see the need to consult with others. Despite the introduction of new machinery, her 23 workers only produced 621 garments a week; in the previous year a workforce of 20 had produced a weekly output of 600 garments.

Narinder's operational targets were to reduce unit costs and improve quality.

The workers had been reluctant to use the off-the-job training she offered, so that they could learn how to use the new machines. They were worried that a day off work would reduce the pay they received through the piecework payment system.

Ineffective use of the machinery meant that many completed garments were rejected by the quality inspectors. On three occasions, Narinder had been forced to order extra materials because of high wastage rates and this was reducing her already low profit margins.

Some poor quality clothing had got through and damaged the company's reputation. Narinder had lost two important contracts with local retailers and orders had fallen sharply from last year, when the factory had been at maximum capacity producing 900 garments a week.

Narinder was unable to achieve her operational targets because of inefficiency in operations management, so she concentrated on improving her marketing. Her new contacts had encouraged her to produce ethnic clothing that could be sold at a higher price. Market research indicated that all of Narinder's garments were selling in low growth markets, with many in the decline stage of the product life cycle. Two 'cash cows' were responsible for 90% of the profits and both of these had needed extension strategies in recent years.

This year

Narinder decided to invest in new ethnic products that could achieve high value added. Within a year, ten new products were launched. Some struggled in the fast-growing, very competitive markets, but four new products were showing excellent sales levels.

Unfortunately, the heavy expenses involved in launching new products were leading to cash-flow problems. At first these new products were funded by the profits that Narinder had retained, but now she was running out of cash — just at the time when everything looked so promising. However, she had an excellent relationship with the bank manager, having paid back any loans promptly. Her suppliers were keen for her to succeed as she always paid immediately and the shops that she supplied liked the fact that she gave them three months to pay.

Narinder was on the brink of success but urgently needed to improve her cash flow.

(a) **Using the data in paragraph 2, show that labour productivity has fallen since the previous year.** (5 marks)

(b) **Analyse two factors that might have led to Narinder being unable to reach her operational targets.** (8 marks)

(c) **Discuss the extent to which Narinder is using product portfolio analysis in her marketing.** (13 marks)

(d) **Evaluate the methods that Narinder might employ in order to improve her cash flow.** (14 marks)

Answer to Case Study 6: candidate A

(a) labour productivity per week = $\dfrac{\text{output (number of garments per week)}}{\text{number of employees}}$

Previous year: $\dfrac{600 \text{ garments}}{20 \text{ workers}}$ = 30 garments per worker (per week)

This year: $\dfrac{621}{23}$ = 27

Therefore labour productivity per week has fallen from 30 garments per worker to 27 garments per worker.

> Excellent calculations that earn full marks. In the second calculation the candidate has abbreviated the detail to include just the numbers. Under pressure of time this is fine, as long as the candidate does not lose sight of the eventual measurement. In this case it is 27 garments per worker per week and not just '27'. The fact that this detail was put into the first calculation has probably helped Candidate A to keep a focus on the measurement. It is a common error to present an answer as a number without indicating whether it is garments, pounds, units or perhaps even thousands of units.

(b) Operational targets include unit costs, quality and capacity utilisation.

Narinder should be able to meet these targets because she is achieving high value added. With high levels of profit, we can assume that unit costs will increase and so this increase will help to achieve the operational target.

Capacity utilisation can also be achieved as she is increasing the number of workers from 20 to 23.

> Candidate A earns credit in the opening line for recognising 'operational targets', although they are not explained. In paragraph 2 the answer is not addressing the question, as there is no direct connection between high levels of profit and unit costs. Furthermore, the target for unit costs will normally be a decrease and so

the increase in unit cost noted in the answer would not be helping to achieve an operational target. The final paragraph also shows a misunderstanding of capacity utilisation. It is the 'actual output as a percentage of maximum possible output'. The candidate needed to focus on the number of garments produced and relate this to the maximum capacity of 900, noted in paragraph 4 of the article, rather than looking at the number of employees. Overall this answer did not show any real understanding of the question set, but did earn credit for the opening definition.

(c) Narinder used product portfolio analysis a lot in her marketing. Product portfolio analysis looks at the range of products produced by a particular organisation. There are two main tools of product portfolio analysis — the product life cycle and the Boston matrix. There is evidence that Narinder used both.

Her market research indicated that she was selling in low growth markets, with many products in decline. Consequently these products probably had low market shares. They would be classified as dogs within the Boston matrix. Narinder realised that she needed to get rid of these dogs and introduce new products into growing markets. By diversifying into ethnic products with high added value and growing markets, she was trying to establish potential stars (or possibly problem children, as they would start with a low market share).

Narinder also used extension strategies to support two cash cows — proof that she recognised the importance of the Boston matrix in her strategy.

Narinder also used the product life cycle, recognising that there were many products in the decline stage of their life cycle. She used the profit from the cash cows to start launching new products. Ten new products were launched into fast growing, competitive markets. Four of these new products were showing promising sales in their first year and were in the growth stage of the life cycle — a very promising achievement.

In conclusion I would say that Narinder used both tools of product portfolio analysis in a very effective way. She used the Boston matrix in order to decide which products to delete and which ones to use to fund new products. She used the product life cycle to try to overcome the problem facing the business, whereby it had too many declining products and none experiencing growth. Within two years she transformed the business into one with four excellent new growing products.

This is a very strong answer. Candidate A has shown an excellent understanding of the concept of product portfolio analysis. He/she has then taken this theory and applied it to the events within the article in a very mature manner. The excellent combination of analysis and application is underpinned throughout by judgement shown in selecting the appropriate theory. This evaluation is further enhanced by the conclusion which summarises the extent to which product portfolio analysis has helped Narinder in her marketing. This response would have earned a very high mark, especially when taking into account the level of difficulty of this question.

(d) There are a number of ways in which Narinder might have improved her cash flow:
- a bank overdraft
- a short-term loan
- debt factoring
- sale of assets
- sale and leaseback of assets
- selling more products
- using profits

With the high growth in sales of the new products, I think Narinder should be able to make money from her profit in order to improve the business's cash flow. With four new products all growing fast, there should be a big inflow of cash that Narinder could use.

Narinder might be able to get a short-term loan from the bank and use it to buy whatever assets the business needs.

After looking at the case study, I think it is more likely that an overdraft would be a good solution to her difficulties. She is running out of cash just at the time when everything is looking promising. She has an excellent relationship with her bank manager. It is almost certain that she could prove to the bank manager that any overdraft would be repaid quite quickly. A bank loan, however, would not be appropriate because the heavy expenses involved in launching the new products have mostly been incurred at the time of her recognising the need to boost her cash flow. She cannot use retained profits to solve the cash-flow problems as, according to the case study, she is now running out of cash from this source.

Narinder's suppliers were keen for her to succeed as she paid them immediately. This may be the cause of her cash-flow problem. She could negotiate credit terms with her suppliers and delay payments. This would enable her to overcome a cash shortage.

At present she is giving the shops that she supplies three months to pay. She could get hold of this money immediately by debt factoring. A factoring company would buy these debts from her and give her an immediate payment of a large percentage of the debt. Narinder may not need to do this permanently. The article suggests that she is suffering from a temporary cash-flow shortage — in the long term she may not want to use debt factoring as it would lose her money.

Finally, Narinder should consider the factory. If she owns the factory, she could sell and lease it back — this would give her a large sum of money. Because she is working well below capacity, it might be possible for her to sell off part of the factory. However, as the business is now growing again this may not be a sensible strategy. On balance I would not advise Narinder to use either of these methods as she will lose ownership of a major asset in order to overcome a short-term problem that could be sorted out much more simply.

In conclusion I would recommend that Narinder negotiates a bank overdraft and arranges to factor the debts that she is owed by the shops that she supplies. She should also try to negotiate some credit from her suppliers — she appears to be a very good customer and they would want to keep her goodwill.

> ✐ This answer starts unconvincingly. Candidate A shows that he/she knows the various methods of overcoming a cash-flow problem, although the final two bullet points are ways of making profit rather than specifically suited to resolving a short-term cash-flow problem. After this list, paragraphs 2 and 3 show limited analysis.
>
> However, the answer suddenly improves at the beginning of paragraph 4. The candidate appears to have looked into the case study in order to get some ideas — an excellent strategy. From that point onwards, the answer takes on a whole new level, as every argument is rooted firmly in the context of the case study. The answer shows excellent evaluation skills in weighing up the relative merits of different solutions to this problem. Candidate A shows great maturity in sifting out those solutions that will not help the business in the long term, while focusing on those that relate most appropriately to the situation in which Narinder finds her business: a short-term cash-flow problem that, if overcome, will allow the business to become much more successful.

> ✐ **A solid A-grade response. There are three excellent answers, each achieving full marks. Question (b) has been misread or misunderstood, but some credit was given for the definitions. Answering the high mark questions very well will assure an A grade is achieved by the candidate.**

Answer to Case Study 6: candidate B

(a) Labour productivity: last year = $\dfrac{20}{600}$ = 30 garments per week

this year = $\dfrac{23}{621}$ = 27 garments per week

Therefore productivity has fallen by 3 garments per week.

> ✐ The candidate has achieved the correct answers, even though the figures are inverted in the formula. Benefit of the doubt is given to the candidate and he/she achieves full marks.

(b) Narinder's operating targets were 900 garments per week and good quality clothing being produced. She was unable to reach her target of 900 garments because orders have declined due to poorer quality products being produced. Customers will stop buying products from a company if they are of poor quality and they can get better quality elsewhere. And if customer orders start to decline, there is little point in carrying on producing such high numbers of goods.

Quality has been poor because staff have refused training on new machinery and this has led to more errors and wastage as they don't know how to do the work properly. If garments are not made properly, quality is bound to fall.

> The candidate shows clear knowledge of operational targets and has applied two of these well to the case study. The answer has been developed to gain the analysis marks awarded for this question. A good response.

(c) Product portfolio analysis is all about dogs, cash cows, stars and problem children, and shows the link between market growth and market share. All the products are selling in low growth markets at the decline stage of the product life cycle and should be eliminated. Therefore she is obviously not using the strategy. We are told she has two cash cows. This is where market share and market growth are both high and she has used extension strategies to extend the life of the product life cycle, so she is using the strategy here.

> The candidate mentions the elements of the Boston matrix and mentions the link to market growth and share but doesn't show any understanding of which element corresponds to these factors. Information has been lifted from the case study and an attempt has been made to apply it, but the candidate's lack of knowledge is evident when the description of a cash cow is wrong. There is some very limited judgement about products not being removed from sale. The marks awarded here are low as the candidate lacks knowledge about the key terms in the question.

(d) Narinder can use lots of methods to improve her cash flow. She can use an overdraft from the bank for temporary cash shortages. Loans can be used, where money is again borrowed from a bank and paid back with interest over time. She could sell off assets and gain the money and then either keep that money or lease back the assets at a fixed rate per annum. She could obtain raw materials on credit from suppliers to help cash flow, or she could debt factor and sell off her debts to a debt factor and gain the cash immediately.

We are told that she has an excellent relationship with the bank and pays back loans quickly, so she could either take out another loan which would be paid back with interest or she could take out an overdraft which she would only have to use if the need arose. Either of these would help her with temporary cash shortages.

She could also demand payment up front for goods, rather than allowing shops three months to pay as she does at the moment. However, as they are used to having credit, she may lose these customers. Perhaps she could instead offer discounts for payments for goods on delivery instead which would help her cash flow.

📝 The candidate has a very sound knowledge of the methods of improving cash flow, as shown in the first paragraph. However, too much time has probably been spent on this section and the candidate would be better advised to apply the scenario into the theory at the same time, rather than returning to the methods as he/she has in the second paragraph and then explaining them again in the context of the case study. The third paragraph is applied well to the scenario and analysis and evaluation is present.

📝 **This is a B/C response. There are good answers to questions (a), (b) and (d), although question (d) would have benefited from application as the points were raised, as time has been lost in developing and evaluating the points made in sufficient depth. The candidate struggles due to the lack of knowledge in question (c). If this had been present, the marks for this question would have been a lot higher.**